Fisherman's Spring

RODERICK HAIG-BROWN

Fisherman's

Spring

Illustrated by Louis Darling

Nick Lyons Books

Printed in the United States of America

10 9 8 7 6 5 4 3 2 1

Library of Congress Cataloging-in-Publication Data

Haig-Brown, Roderick Langmere, 1908–1976.
  Fisherman's spring.

  1. Fly fishing.   I. Title.
SH451.H197   1988   799.1′1   88-572
ISBN 0-941130-74-6

Preface to the 1975 Edition

A fisherman's seasons are not that much different from those of any other outdoor observer except that they are focused on water—rivers and lakes, ponds and streams, and the sea. In a world of great and varied beauty, nothing is more beautiful than water, especially moving water. I am aware of the beauty of water frozen into glaciers and icebergs, their immensity and power and the glorious lights that the sun can summon from them. I have again and again admired the breathless early morning calm on lakes large and small and the reflection of the hills about them. The power of ocean storms and the glory of ocean surf in sunlight have a magnificence beyond almost anything. Besides these splendors, the intimacy of a fisherman's river may seem a slight thing. Yet I think that flowing water in all its forms is most beautiful of all.

There are large rivers and small rivers, rough rivers and quiet ones. I am not thinking of the sweeping calm of the lower reaches of great rivers like the Fraser and the St. Lawrence, nor of the wild fury of such places as Hell's Gate in the Fraser Canyon, though these places too have meaning for fishermen. I am thinking chiefly of fly-fishing streams, clear-water, cool-water streams, not too large and formidable for intimacy. Every fisherman has several of these in his mind and memory; they are his special places and he knows the cycle of their seasons.

Perhaps the seasons are no more strongly marked along the streams than anywhere else. Plant growth springs, flourishes, falls into dormancy everywhere: the different birds come and go, the earth is warm or cold, there is snowfall and freeze-up, snow melt and the new warmth of the new season's sun in Central Park or on city streets, in farmland or woodland as well as along streams. But along streams I think there is a special intensity. Life concentrates there; successions and contrasts are more dramatic. Insect life is especially rich and summons other life to its abundance. Nothing is more sharply and obviously seasonal than the runs of anadromous fish, especially the salmon's, and these too bring other life to focus on the streams. Even in winter, so long as there is open water, there is life about the streams and in them too.

Whether or not a fisherman's seasons are more blessed than those of others matters little. Certainly they contain life and change and excitement enough to fill many books. So these are four books of one fisherman's seasons, originally written and published over ten or twelve years of seasons and now returned to print in a single year. They could be written again and undoubtedly will be, by other fishermen, of other seasons. For there are always new ways of seeing, new ways of remembering, and new ways of telling about it all. One hopes only that the seasons themselves will not change, nor the waters that respond to them.

Roderick Haig-Brown
October, 1974

Contents

Fisherman's Spring

The Art of Fishing

IN STARTING A NEW FISHING BOOK I have an uneasy feeling that I ought to protect myself with some such graceful apology as came so easily to Milton's pen when he began to write *Lycidas*. I have already written a lot about fish and fishing, and perhaps I have nothing new to say. Certainly I am not impressed with myself when I read the books of other fishermen and realize what effort and devotion they spend on their experiments and research and on just plain fishing. My trouble is that I am a writer first and a fisherman second. I go fishing quite a lot and I think about fishing a lot, but I write all the time. A writer doesn't freely choose what he writes about; he writes what is in him and of him, and he writes what he thinks people will want to read. I know people want to read about fishing because they tell me they do; I usually want to say something about fishing, because pleasant and interesting and satisfying things happen to me whenever I go fishing. So the result is a fishing book every so often. This one is three or four years, and three or four books, after the last one.

I devoutly believe that a healthy man's work should be the most important thing in his life, but I believe just as strongly that no man's keenest interest should be limited to the narrow specialization of his work. If it is he is something less than a man, living something less than a life.

The sport of fishing is an important part of life to many thousands of people, perhaps several millions of people, on this continent alone. It needs no more than this to make it an important subject. But it is also something more than a sport. It is intimate exploration of a part of the world hidden from the eyes and minds of ordinary people. It is a way of thinking and doing, a way of reviving the mind and body, that men have been following with growing intensity for hundreds of years. Fishing has contributed much to the minds of statesmen and Supreme Court justices, college presidents and philosophers, auto workers, pulp mill workers, real estate men, medical men, storekeepers, scientists, railroad engineers and lawyers; in turn, they and many others have contributed to the sport until it has become an art, ephemeral, graceful, complicated, full of tradition yet never static. It is as much a part of modern civilization as most of the minor arts and sciences and probably has more direct effect on more lives than any of them.

I am concerned to write of fishing in these terms, broadly, critically and sometimes technically, with little thought of teaching or discovering new things except out of old things. I am not an innovator or a revolutionary; I prefer growth in continuity along traditional lines. Nor am I an expert or an authority on anything connected with fish or fishing; the field is too broad for that, the imponderables too numerous, the important qualities of the art are too elusive and too dependent upon individual human responses. It is possible, I suppose, by taking much thought and much practice, to become expert in the biology of fishes and the entomology of streams, or in the varied arts and crafts of casting, fly-tying, rod-building, bait-cutting and so forth, but I have never done so. I have simply gone fishing, enjoyed fishing and followed occasionally the compulsions of aroused curiosity, or sought to alleviate the discomforts of inadequate technique. Not unnaturally, the fish themselves have done most to arouse my curiosity. So I have watched them and read about them and thought about them and may, from time to time, have learned something useful about them. Because a comfortable competence in technique is a necessary prerequisite to the higher enjoyment of any art or sport, I have become reasonably proficient in casting, in making flies, in tying on leaders, greasing lines, cleaning fish and other such incidentals; but nothing is farther from my conception of the sport than to compete in any of these things, or in the more obvious matter of catching fish, with my brother anglers. I go fishing to please myself, not to catch my breakfast or prove anything or enter into any conflict.

If the past of fishing as a sport and an art interests me, its present and future in both aspects interest me still more. There has been a close and continuous history of development, excellently recorded in a voluminous literature, through the past five or six hundred years. The sport as we now have it is at something approaching full flower, technically as perfect as it needs to be, but still open to infinite creative interpretation. Its future is in the hands of the enormous numbers of men and women who now have leisure and opportunity to pursue it. They have to carry it into a new phase that will somehow combine protective limitations with the expansive ideas of a new continent. That can only be done through a deep and thorough understanding and an inspired use of the sport's intangible values, and it will be an interesting process. Still more interesting will be some future historian's assessment of the place and effect of the sport in the first civilization to offer its citizens abundant leisure and a secure old age.

The purpose of this book is simply to entertain—specifically, to entertain in that brief moment of relaxation between the end of a day's work and the start of a night's sleep. I have designed it that way because many fishing friends and acquaintances and correspondents have asked me to. Several have asked for a fishing almanac, day by day and dated through the year. I explored the idea thoroughly and even wrote a sample month or two. The form has many pleasant features, but it makes for a long book, heavy to hold and expensive to produce, and it has inherent dangers of monotony and strain that it seems wise to avoid.

To entertain, in its highest sense of providing sustenance for the mind, is the most important purpose a writer can have. I know that much of my own pleasure in fishing is in the flowing ease of thought that comes upon me as I fish. This is compounded of many things; of companionship or solitude, of a river's moods and changes, a bird's flight, a fish's leap, a lake's calm or stir. It grows from wind and weather and season, from theories built and tried, from endless curiosity and the constant expectancy that goes with fishing. It is made smoother and easier by the mechanical efficiency of sensible tackle and a moderate skill in casting and wading. It is broadened by a decent knowledge of the ways of water and fish and the creatures fish depend on, as well as by the whole frame of reference that is a man's mind. These are the things I mean to put in my book. If it becomes didactic anywhere, or too solemn, or useful in any practical way—well, the stream must have been running too pleasantly, the casting too easy, the time between rises too long; my thoughts got ahead of me.

Spring Defined

A FISHERMAN'S SPRING MUST START, I think, with the opening of the trout season. Here, on the coast of British Columbia, that is March first. It goes on through April and May into June, spring rather than summer so long as snow is melting freely away from the mountainsides, so long as the leaves on the trees are fresh green, still growing, and air and earth are still moist, sunlight still washed and bright and dust-free.

Spring is the movement of stonefly nymphs in the fast water and the hatching of the first stoneflies. It is the stirring of salmon alevins up through the gravel, their emergence into huddled clumps still vaguely orange from the partially absorbed yolk sacs, their spread through the river as fry and the flight of most of them to salt water through a gauntlet of trout and mergansers, bullheads and loons and kingfishers and their own yearling relatives. It is in the slow warming of the lakes, in the steady increase of the rivers as the snow comes off, in rain showers and mayfly hatches, in occasional days of storm and bitter wind more savagely chilling than the worst of winter, other days of flashing life and color more brilliant than summer's richest. Spring is bloom of dog-tooth violet and trilliums along the flood-swept river banks, it is in the scarlet of the sapsucker's breast, the flight of bandtail pigeons, the return of the yellow warblers to alders and willows overhanging the water. It is geese nesting on the little lakes, mallards paired on the beaver ponds, frogs croaking in the swamps. It is rediscovery of pools and shallows changed or unchanged by a winter of weather, sudden freedom from the heavier gear of winter fishing, freedom from the restraints of snow and ice and short days; it is the whole promise of a new season ahead and the new pleasures that one knows will come, all unexpected, from the familiar sport of going out beside water with a rod.

I have written before that I do not believe in British Columbia's March opening of the trout season. It exposes our good cutthroats too soon, before they have finished their spawning and certainly before they have had time to get back to the comparative safety of saltwater feeding. It is also an extra and unnecessary month added on to a season already far too long for the happy future of the natural stock of fish. Few fishermen would miss it and few have it in most other parts of the world.

But since the season is open I usually do go trout fishing at least a few times in March, and nearly always find some special pleasure in it. This year, which is 1950, March was cold and wintry as it can be, with rough winds and sleet and the snow melting swiftly away from the lower levels. There was a good run of fresh steelhead early in the month, small silvery fish of six or seven pounds, and I fished for them with a big single-handed rod and smaller flies than I use through most of the winter. I was still fishing for them when I found the early cutthroats.

I had come through the Nameless Pool with a No. 4 Golden Girl, bright and handsome on 9/5 gut, smaller than my usual winter flies, a concession to the lighter rod, though the water was strong enough and high enough to suggest a 2/0 fly and heavier gut. The upper lie was blank, but a bright six-pounder took the fly when I was a few feet below the big rock. He fought me hard, jumping a lot and running well against the strong water of the rapid, but I went in with him at last and it was over. It was what I wanted and what I had expected. I have never caught a fresh-run steelhead below that second lie in the Nameless Pool, and wading in the heavy water among the great round boulders of the bottom is difficult and thoroughly uncomfortable. I should have gone home.

Instead of that, I went out into the water again. I may have been thinking of trout, but more probably I was following the obstinate and suspicious nature that will never let me trust my knowledge of a pool. No matter how many times I have fished good-looking water without result, I always feel bound to try a fly through it again when I come to it, if only to prove to myself that nothing has changed. So I started from where I had hooked my fish and worked on down.

Half a dozen casts later a fish took me, deep, on the swing, for all the world like a steelhead. He went away strongly, upstream from the pull of the line, and I still thought he was a steelhead. Then he jumped and I saw a two-pound trout. I treated him contemptuously, of course, started towards shore too soon, found myself giving line and watching a series of jumps that convinced me I had an early fish from the May run of rainbows. I let him run me under a sunken limb and was lucky to bring him free from it. When I got him on the bank I found he was a cutthroat, perfect in shape, handsomely colored, as worthy a spring fish as I have ever taken.

The Golden Girl rose me a second fish in almost the same place a few minutes later, a fraction larger than the first one but his twin in color and condition. I wondered why they should have bothered with a bright orange fly worked slow and deep for steelhead. When I opened the first fish I thought it was all explained— his belly was full of steelhead eggs from an early spawner. So I opened the second for confirmation and found stonefly nymphs, mayfly nymphs, a drowned beetle, many caddis grubs, anything and everything but steelhead eggs. I had the grace, at that moment, to wonder why I ever presume to theorize about the way of a trout with a fly.

It was a more than usually satisfactory opening of the trout season. Far too often I have gone out with 2x and a No. 6 fly, to fasten the second or third cast into a powerful steelhead of ten or twelve pounds. Many times I have gone up to find the river seemingly empty of everything except February spawners, as it logically should be since the fry are not yet moving and there is little to tempt clean fish up from the tidal water. Many times I have gone to some distant lake to find it bleak and cold and unpromising, whether or not the trout were moving.

The surest and safest place to start looking for trout

in early March on a coast stream would be in the tidal water. The fish are clean there and strong and feeding, if one can find them. But in the tidal water there is no closed season, so there can be no opening. Perhaps the best way of all is not to select, not to go out with the avowed intention of catching a March trout just because the season is open, but to let it happen. Sooner or later in the month will come a day when the river looks right for a certain pool, when the weather seems too fresh and inviting to stay home, or when one has a sudden hunch for this lake that was early one year or the little stream where the stonefly hatch is strong or the beaver dam slough where the water warms quickly. If the hunch proves itself one has learned something. If it doesn't, one has still stolen another day from all the days that slip by with rods in their cases and reels silent.

Figures and Definitions

SOME OF MY MORE CASUAL ANGLING friends, or non-angling friends who for some reason read my fishing books, grow quite angry with me for using fishing terms that are not clear to them. Anglers do have a rather involved technical language of their own, and perhaps we toss it about too freely. We also change it and think up new stuff and half the time, unless we are inveterate readers of the question and answer columns of the sporting magazines, we don't altogether know each other's meaning—and hesitate to ask for fear of showing our ignorance.

I, for instance, don't know what is meant by a "parabolic" rod. Interested friends have explained it to me, but I'm afraid there's something mathematical in it and can never bear to listen properly. Such "parabolic" rods as I have handled seem to me very powerful for their weight, quite heavy in the tip, and with the main driving action well forward. And that's about as far as I intend to go into the matter.

There is also a type of fly called an "optic." No one has ever explained this to me, but I have some of them and the main point about them seems to be that they are tied with a big round head which has the semblance of an eye painted on it or set into it—hence, presumably, optic; though it's hard to believe. The first flies of this type I ever saw were coho salmon patterns given to me by Bill Boeing back in the thirties, and we didn't call them optics then.

I have talked along cheerfully in this book about such things as hair flies, strip-wing, built-wing and hackle flies. By "hair flies" I mean flies whose wing is made mostly of hair—deer, bear, fox, goat, gopher, badger or what you will. And the hair may be tied along the shank of the hook, as in a wet fly, or at an angle to it, as in a dry fly. "Strip wings" are made from narrow strips of joined fibers cut from the feather of a bird—mallard, teal, wigeon, swan, bustard, pheasant and so on. A "built wing" is one in which strips from one or more different feathers are united into a single strip. By "hackle fly" I usually mean a dry fly which has, in place of wings, a cock's hackle folded and wound round the hook so that the fibers stick straight out. The term can also be applied to a wet fly, but in this case a feather with soft and flexible hackles is usually chosen, and it is tied so that the fibers lie somewhat back along the hook-shank. One might also speak of a whole hackle wet fly, which would normally be a streamer-type with long, tapering hackles taking the place of strip wings.

Sizes are another trouble—of lines and leaders and flies. Quite a bad trouble too, because the same sizes don't always mean the same things. Leader sizes are fairly standard and seem to apply equally to nylon or gut. Seven one-thousandths of an inch is the diameter of 4x gut, with a theoretical breaking strain of 1¼ lbs. From there the sizes increase, by one one-thousandth of an inch at each step, through 3x, 2x, 1x to 0x. Then, for some reason I wouldn't know, the designation changes to 9/5, though the significance is still an increase in diameter of one one-thousandth. From there the numbers go down again through 8/5, 7/5 and so on to 0/5, which probably breaks at around 20 lbs. and has a diameter of twenty-one one-thousandths. The heaviest gut I use is 3/5, for winter steelheads, and the lightest I use is 4x.

Hook sizes are complicated by at least two sets of numbers, known as "old" and "new" numbers. So far as I know, only the "old" series is used in North America. It runs from 20 to 1 in ascending order of magnitude, then changes to 1/0, 2/0 and so on up to 10/0, which is the largest fly hook I have seen. A No.

18 fly, which is very tiny, is tied on a hook 7/32″ long. From size 20 to 14, the variation is 1/32″. From 14 to 4 it is by sixteenths. And from there on by eighths. A No. 10 hook is 9/16″ long, a No. 6 is 13/16″, a No. 1 is 1¼″, a No. 2/0 is 1 5/8″. The new numbers are used mainly in England and go upwards from 000, which is 17, to No. 9, which is No. 6. I don't know why, and I wish I had never known about it.

Fly-line sizes, again for no reason known to me, have the same jerk in the middle that gut sizes and hook sizes have. And the English sizes don't mean the same as the American sizes. On the whole, it is a very unpleasant subject and I don't think I will go into it much. The size refers to the diameter of the line and is usually expressed by a letter, from I, which is light and thin (twenty to twenty-four one-thousandths of an inch) up to B, which seems to be forty-eight one-thousandths in England and fifty-five one-thousandths in America. Beyond B one is really coming into salmon sizes. America goes up through the A's—2A, 3A and so on. England goes down through numbers, 6, 5, 4, etc., to 1. A tapered line is described by the thickness of its belly and its two ends—GBG, for instance, or HCH. Multiple tapers lead to things like GB2AG and worse. Fortunately the manufacturers gave up when they came to seven-taper lines and just used numbers; so nobody knows just what they mean. The only thing is to take a line and try it out with the rod it is supposed to fit. Which is true of most rods and most lines.

Glib talk of fly lines, even apart from sizes, can make plenty of trouble and confusion. We fishermen are likely to go cheerfully on about double-tapered lines, torpedo heads, level lines, vacuum-dressed lines, without the slightest thought as to whether anyone can understand us or whether we ourselves know what we are talking about. Vacuum-dressed, for instance; I know that the best fly lines for years have advertised themselves as made of "vacuum-dressed silk" and I suppose that means the dressing is put on the silk in a vacuum. It might also mean by a vacuum or through a vacuum or perhaps nothing to do with a vacuum, especially since I have often heard the process referred to as "the secret of vacuum dressing." All I know is that the process produces a good result.

The thickness, which also represents the weight and air resistance, of a line is of great importance to a fly-fisherman. For any sort of effective fly-fishing the line must be matched to the rod—that is, of a proper weight to draw out its power and action. A line which tapers in thickness from its main part towards its end is on the whole more effective and more delicate in use than a line that is level from end to end. A double-tapered line is one whose main thickness tapers at both ends through some fifteen or twenty feet to become four or five sizes finer. This leaves fifty or sixty feet of working line or belly in the normal thirty-yard line. The point of having the taper at both ends is simply that the line can be reversed when the dressing becomes worn.

Torpedo-head lines usually have some fifteen feet of very heavy belly, tapering through ten feet to a point at the front end, and through ten feet to a long length of fine-running line at the back end. The idea of this is to enable the caster to "shoot" a long length of running line through the sharp pull of the short length of heavy line at the end of his cast. It works. Multiple tapers do the same thing more scientifically and more effectively through gradations of taper designed to enable the caster to carry a maximum of line with his cast in the air, and shoot a maximum at the end. Both torpedo heads and multiple tapers are developments of modern tournament casting. Casting with them makes most fishermen look as though they were swatting black flies with broom handles; in fact, it is claimed by those who should know that a good man can cast a multiple-taper line pretty nearly as far with a broom handle as he can with a good rod.

The names of casts can also lead a man quickly into floundering beyond his depth. I try to keep away from all names except the few I do understand. The wind cast, for instance; a friend who is a professional instructor tells me I use it, but I'm sure I can't describe it. One does drive a cast into a strong wind by a certain delayed application of force, and perhaps that's what it is. The switch cast, I'm told, is wonderfully effective. I've tried to learn it from books and diagrams, but am still no wiser than I was. It seems to be a roll that puts the fly out at an angle to the line of recovery, and I can do this quite comfortably, though what I do doesn't seem to be what the books tell me to do, nor is it as effective as they claim. Casts like the spey and double-spey, I think I understand, and I have tried to describe them elsewhere in this book. I have also mentioned such casts as the angle, the steeple and the shepherd's crook, all too casually I'm afraid. "Angle" is a name of my own for an overhead cast in which the back cast or recovery is made parallel to the bank, the delivery at right angles to it. In a steeple cast, the back cast is thrown as nearly as possible straight up into the air, to clear bushes behind; the forward cast, theoretically, shoots out in fine shape as though the back cast had been made in the ordinary way. For me, it usually doesn't. The shepherd's crook throws the line in just that shape, with the leader in a curve like a query, to bring a dry fly over the fish ahead of any attachment. I know it sounds an unlikely performance, but it works out surprisingly well.

One shouldn't, in any case, be too much overawed by technical jargon of any kind. What matters about 4x gut is that it is fine enough for the trout to have trouble seeing it, and for the fisherman to have trouble landing the trout he has fooled with it—not that it is seven one-thousandths of an inch in diameter. I confidently expect to go to my grave in ignorance of the meaning of some of the terms my brother anglers use— partly from laziness, partly from shyness, and partly because it doesn't matter very much, anyway. But I enjoy the talk and I like the stuff it refers to.

Fry Imitations

THE COLD, SLOW TIMES OF EARLY spring always turn one's thoughts to stirring trout by imitations of the small fish they feed on. On the Pacific Coast particularly there is the thought of the salmon fry hatches, though here in British Columbia these are not usually of full importance until well on in April.

Fry imitation is somewhere on the ragged edge of respectability in the fly-fisherman's world. It has no proper place on lake or stream where really good hatches of natural insects expose the fish to more orthodox representations, except possibly as a means of persuading a few large fish that seldom or never move to surface feed. From a convinced fly-fisherman's point of view, it is taking advantage of a trout's baser reactions. Yet gear and method remain essentially the same as in other forms of fly-fishing; it is completely logical when and where fry and forage fish are a major item of the trout's concern, and it presents a maze of problems all its own that are fully worthy of any good fisherman's attention.

Every year, towards the end of the steelhead season, I tie up a dozen or so experimental fry imitations. I rarely make two of them exactly the same and I let myself be guided in choice of materials chiefly by thoughts that have come to me in the past year's fishing; confirmations, adjustments or failures of older theories. And I depend on this dozen or so of queer creatures to carry through another year of the vague, evolutionary process by which I am trying to persuade myself to settle to fewer patterns. The method is quite unscientific, and the advance is usually slow because most of the patterns seem to do equally well. By the end of each season I have lost nearly all of them, either by leaving them in fish or giving them away, and have forgotten the exact dressings. But there has been some advance, or at least some change, over the years, because the fly I should tie now as a general purpose imitation is markedly different from the one I did tie ten years ago or five years ago.

When I tie up this annual collection I am thinking first of the early spring trout in the lakes, the larger fish that stir through the cold water for bullheads and sticklebacks, but seldom for lesser, active creatures. After these I am thinking of the cutthroats during the spring hatch in the salmon waters. And after these again the harvest cutthroats and the early running coho salmon in September. So there is range enough for the imagination to work in and ample excuse for varying the patterns.

I used to try to imitate the mottled gray back and dirty white belly of the bullhead. I now think that to do so is a waste of time. Bullheads are a major food supply of practically all large trout in practically all Vancouver Island lakes and streams. But they are essentially bottom fish, stirring in the mud or darting intermittently among the stones, and it seems most unlikely that any fisherman would be able or anxious to imitate this form of movement with his fly.

Sticklebacks are much more promising. They hold in mid-water. They often swim slowly near the surface. They dart in jerking dashes either in mid-water or near the surface. All these movements are easily reproduced by the fly-fisherman and they interest big trout in the early part of the season in a way that nothing else does.

Trout that go after sticklebacks do not sink back into contemplative pose on spotting one, counting the spines, estimating the tapered body form, the curve at the tail, the stiff and slightly awkward swimming movements, the showy colors and pugnacious attitude, before striking. Rather, I imagine the eye catches the movement of a roughly familiar shape, the body responds instantly in violent reflex action, and that is the end of the stickleback unless he is a very fast fish. So flies of many kinds are likely to produce results. A silver doctor will; so will almost any silver-bodied fly of about the right size worked fairly actively at about the right depth. The question is whether any one fly of this general type will produce appreciably better results than the others. Quite frankly, I am not sure. So many complicated factors enter into any experiment under actual fishing conditions, and results are so likely to vary from day to day, that I don't suppose I ever shall be sure.

Unquestionably the most important factors in this, and most other forms of fishing, are where the fisherman puts the fly and how he works it. Action is probably the most important single factor in fishing a minnow fly and can make the difference between getting a rise and not getting one or between getting a short rise and striking into a solid take.

What one wants from the fish is an uninhibited reflex action, an immediate movement to the fly on sight and a completely confident take. Lively evasive action by the fly or some flaw in the reflexes of the fish may cause him to miss, but if his attack is really uninhibited this should only stimulate him to a more accurate second attempt; and if the action of the fly has been good, it is reasonable to assume that there is something wrong with the appearance of the fly.

The early season stickleback is likely to be a dark little fish, developing towards the reds and blues of the

28

breeding season. There is also green in his general coloration and a fair brightness of belly and lower sides. No fish, not even an erudite and objectively-minded old brown trout, is going to analyze all this. But every fish has been comfortably rewarded many times by responding promptly to the general impression of it all. The least the hopeful angler can do is attempt to reproduce this impression.

I am inclined to dispense with the customary silver body in imitating sticklebacks. Silk or wool of very light green and a good blue seem better; I have used gantron for the purpose and found it perfectly good, though there is no way of knowing whether or not it is more effective than conventional materials; on dark days or in evening light it might be. I think a claret hackle is good, with a wing of dyed bear fur, quite sparse, the color mixed—orange, blue, green and yellow or olive.

I know that this dressing is effective, that it catches fish convincingly and consistently. I caught fish well under the same conditions before I thought of the dressing and no doubt could do so again without it. But when I go out to fish for trout in early spring, in a lake full of three-spined sticklebacks, I like now to have some approximation of this fly with me. Whether or not it conveys a convincing impression to the trout, it is a decently logical attempt to do so.

"Local observations," says a recent scientific paper, "indicate that it takes three or four years for the trout to obtain the habit of eating shiners." This, written of lakes into which shiners had been introduced as forage fish, suggests that a fry representation had better be reasonably accurate. It is not that the fish of these lakes have not been used to taking any kind of small fish at all—they have always fed enthusiastically on their descendant fry—but that it does take them a while, rather a long while, to learn to respond to a new introduction.

"Trout," says Theodore Gordon, "have a wonderful eye for color but a very indifferent notion of form." I am not too well satisfied that the second part of this is true of sunk flies, especially fry imitations. In fact, I should be inclined to set form ahead of color in all flies that are actively worked by the fisherman. I do not mean by this that I like the faithful, stiff-bodied facsimiles one sees of nymphs and larvae and small fish, or even such attempts at representing form as the tied-down wings that many tiers use on minnow flies. All of these are stiff and dead in the water, far less realistic in representing live form than the flexibility and shifting color of free feathers and hair. But I believe that size is important, and shape, and anything that contributes to the impression of swift life that is a small fish.

Probably the British sea trout "terrors" and "demons," tied with two or three small hooks in tandem, are the ultimate in representing the lively flexibility of a small fish. But these flies are a nuisance to make, they do not last well and I think they are too deadly for a self-respecting fly-fisherman to play with. Australian and New Zealand flies, tied with long feathers on rather small ordinary hooks, are lifelike and certainly produce rises, but I have never been able to hook Pacific Coast fish even moderately well on them. Nor do I care for the American streamer hook with a very long shank and rather narrow bend; it makes for an unduly stiff and heavy fly and does not hold fish as well as it should because of the excessive leverage.

The only hook I have found wholly satisfactory is the "low-water" Atlantic salmon hook, a light hook of excellent design, long in the shank but with a bend of perfect proportions and an ideal point and barb. One can tie a very slender and graceful fly on this hook, with a fine head that makes for a minimum of resistance in the water. Out of this comes my own notion of what the form of the fry imitation should be. Provided one has in mind the darting slenderness of the stickleback or of trout and salmon fry, the hook itself will almost inevitably lead to the tying of a good representation.

I have said that I tie up a batch of fry imitations every year, rarely making two of them exactly the same; this is clear enough evidence that I have never found anything that seems to me a wholly satisfactory fly, one that seems to do equally well under all conditions when trout are feeding on fry. Probably there is not such a fly. Perhaps, as Preston Jennings suggests, varying light intensity is the important factor and one must have patterns to match. Perhaps the variations of the small fish themselves are important. Perhaps the movement one gives the fly under an infinity of water conditions is more important than either of these things.

I cannot remember that I have ever tied a minnow fly that did not catch fish, in spite of the extravagant variations I have sometimes played with. But I have gradually discarded nearly all the extravagances, instinctively rather than deliberately, and I notice now that my yearly dozen vary far less than they used to. One or two patterns persist and though I have many times varied the dressings in some slight way I now feel fairly satisfied that they have some real value. The first of these is the Silver Brown, an imitation of coho and cutthroat trout fry. The dressing which I have given in many other writings is very simple: Indian crow tail, silver body, natural red hackle, wings of golden pheasant center-tail strips enclosing orange bear fur. It fishes best in low summer water, when most fry except the cutthroats and cohos have left the river, and at that time should be worked very slowly, just under the surface. It is just as likely to move a ten- or twelve-pound steelhead at such times as a two- or three-pound cutthroat, if steelhead are in the stream.

The second pattern I have clung to, and also described elsewhere, is the Silver Lady. This is an early season fly, effective for feeding trout when spring and dog salmon fry are abundant. So far as I can judge its essentials are the silver body and the wing that combines pale blue with some light barred feather such as teal, wood duck or light mallard. I usually add a badger hackle and a whole feather tail of pale pink or orange.

Ten years ago my experimental patterns were variations somewhat along the general lines of these two patterns. I was concerned also to reproduce the unmarked silver-blue-green of the humpback fry for the many streams in which these are the main hatch. This turned me in the end to dyed polar bear fur, and that is now the preponderant wing material of most of my experimental patterns.

For a humpback imitation my choice is: yellow tail, silver body, yellow hackle, with a wing of mixed blue and green bear fur and a few strands of peacock sword (green herl) set over it. This is an effective fly when the humpback fry are going down in good numbers, and it has also caught fish, including steelhead and coho salmon, for me much later in the season. I should like to find a wing still more brilliantly blue and silver, but I think this fly will always take trout that are feeding on fry or minnows without heavy markings or strong colors.

Which brings me at last to the general pattern. I enjoy experimenting because it gives me an excuse to avoid the monotony of tying exactly the same fly over and over again, and because I always have some ideas that I think should be tested. But it wouldn't distress me too much to be limited to a single fry or minnow imitation provided I could vary the hook size and the quantity of material in the wing. I should choose a pale red or pale orange tail, silver body, small scarlet hackle and a wing of mixed, not layered, bear fur—orange, yellow, blue and green are enough variation, though a few strands of white seem to add life to the whole effect.

Minnow flies are producers of big fish under most conditions and sometimes, especially on the Pacific Coast salmon rivers during the big hatches and movements, they are essential. Pattern probably has bearing on the effectiveness of imitations, but I am sure that movement and depth has much more. A small fish moves much more freely and variably than most subaquatic creatures and its coloration is normally such that the least eccentricity of movement is extremely revealing; so long as the silver belly is straight down, the dark back straight up, the little fish remains fairly hard to see from above or below; a sharp turn, a twist, a wobble, can cause the bright sides and belly to catch light and send a flash through the water. The type of movement is likely to vary with conditions and even species of fish, and presumably the type of the revealing flash varies with that of the movement. Presumably, also, the response of the trout will be readiest to the type of flash that is most nearly characteristic of the fry of the moment. If so, the wise fisherman will not be content with a single way of working his minnow imitation. He will try several.

Sometimes it is possible to call the shot on movement. When the trout are slashing the surface and fry are jumping out ahead of them, a fast strip, high in the water and with intermittent breaks is likely to be as good as anything. In early spring, when there are few fry about, a slow, smooth, deep retrieve may be best. Still earlier, in alevin time, a drifting, rolling fly is worth trying, or a slow and halting movement at depth. In late summer, for the big harvest cutthroats, I like to use pure greased-line method—a slim fly, controlled just under the surface film with a minimum of artificial movement.

There are many other variations and usually one can only find the right one for the particular moment by trial and error. I like to search with a slow fly, worked only a little faster than one works the fly for non-feeding fish; I have the feeling that variations of current will be enough to produce eccentric movement. But until I am satisfied that the fish are taking the slow fly I always vary it with faster movement, jerking movement, smooth movement, or sudden starts of activity. And I try my best to remember, and repeat, what I was doing when the fish took.

Simulating movement in lakes and slack water is harder than in streams, because everything then depends on hand and line. But one can let the fly down to a depth more easily in still water, and there is probably less fear of missing or discouraging fish through working the fly too fast; one knows nearly all the time what is going on. In swift and broken streams it is very easy to hurry a minnow fly too much, either by stripping too fast or by casting too far and too straight downstream. Both depth and speed can be controlled to a considerable extent by the angle of the cast, upstream, downstream or across. In a stream, too, movement of the rod top alone can be made to affect the fly.

As I sit here and write it down, it all sounds fine. But let me admit that there have been times, more than a few of them, when the trout were taking fry all around me and nothing I could do, either by changing the pattern or its movement, tempted them to do more than follow, or rise half-heartedly or boil angrily far short of the hook. Invariably one remembers something, left untried, that might have worked. I remember movement, not pattern.

35

Early Cutthroat Lakes

Vancouver island has an uncount-able number of lakes of all sizes that hold plenty of trout. Many of them are readily accessible by good roads, others are hidden away among the maze of sub-roads, old logging grades, reforestation roads and other such difficult ways, and still others can be reached only on foot. They are not wonderful producers, in the way the alkaline lakes of the interior are, nor do they often yield extremely big fish to the fly. But they provide a lot of pleasant sport for increasing numbers of people, and there is a wonderfully exciting sense of possession in merely knowing that all these lakes are ready and awaiting one's exploration. One can select among them with almost profligate carelessness and be reasonably sure of finding an interesting and satisfying place, at least some fish and, especially in the early part of the season, no one else around.

Most fishermen nowadays go to such lakes with car-top boats, and that is the wise way to go. But I learned the small lake habit in a country without roads and my thought turns first always to the possibilities of wading the edge of the lake or walking out on logs to get at the fish. After that I think of building a raft, packing in a canoe or even a rubber boat; my slow mind has never yet got used to the idea of setting a perfectly good row-boat on car top or trailer and carrying it effortlessly to where I want to fish. I play with the idea, look at suitable boats in catalogues and advertisements, check the advantages and disadvantages of various carrying rigs—then follow my old conservative ways.

My preference is always to fish from the oriented security of my own two feet. And my favorite lake fishing in all the world is at the head of a big northern lake where a wide strong stream comes in over gravel shallows. It is a windy lake and in spring and summer the westerlies build a steep and heavy swell against the river current. The fish are not especially numerous, and they do not rise very freely. But the few that do show are large. Once I hooked a five-pounder there at midday, seeing his back and most of his body arch smoothly out in the sunlit trough of a wave, knowing that he would turn instantly down for the lake and take more line than I cared to give. Another fish, only a fraction smaller, quietly intercepted a big dry fly on the dying, oil-smooth swell of the wind's leaving, in the gleaming red and black light of a sun already behind the mountains. These fish I have remembered and shall remember.

It is not fair to expect such things of the little lakes, but they can hold brilliant moments and sharp surprises. I went first to Harlequin Lake over twenty years ago, when it was still in the virgin timber. I knew it was two or three miles long, fed by a strong stream from a larger lake and that it was cut almost in two by a narrow neck about half a mile above its outlet. But I had not guessed from the map that this neck would be a slow, quiet river, ten or fifteen feet deep and nearly a hundred yards long, flowing between open, gently sloping banks of hardhack and swamp grass. It seemed sometimes that all the feed from the main body of the lake must be funneling into this gentle river and all the fish from the smaller end must be coming up to meet it. Something of the sort was happening the first time I came to the lake and I walked slowly up along the easy bank, covering rise after rise and hooking twelve- to fifteen-inch trout at every cast.

Later in the day I built a raft and on other days I searched the lake, finding the lovely stream at the head and moving good fish all along the shelf and the drop-off, as well as in the first reaches of the stream itself; I found the good shoal in the big bay just above the narrows and the deep place under the bluffs, where trout came mysteriously out of darkness, up and up through twenty or thirty feet of blue-green water to take a dry fly twitched along the surface. But there was no place better or more rewardingly interesting than the slow, dead-straight stretch of moving water, not quite river, not quite lake, that joined the lake's two sections. It was not always full of rising fish or full of fish at all. But there were always fish there and I learned that it was well worth waiting and watching for bigger ones than the fifteen-inchers I had caught on the first day.

Cordulia Lake is almost round, with an island in the middle and no inlet or outlet that I have ever found, though I have waded clear around its half-mile of shore-line. It is full of trout and full of every kind of feed, especially dragonfly and damsel fly larvae. I trust to these especially in the early part of the season, sinking a big fly (Kerry's Special of the long flexible pheasant tail strands for preference) well down and working it up and along in explosive jerks until an equally explosive jerk in the opposite direction warns me to let things go. Cordulia will do better than this; as the season goes on the fish come nobly to the surface and slash at dry flies with an unsophisticated boldness that no amount of releasing from barbless hooks has so far tamed. But it is an early lake, warming so quickly at the surface that the trout seek the cool depths near the springs by the first or second week of June and stay there through the summer, while the dragon nymphs climb out on the logs, shuck their skins and fill the air with the flickering and rustling of their intricate flight.

Cordulia must once have been a part of Cranefly Lake, before the narrow neck of land which separates the two built up and began to grow brush and trees. Cranefly really is a boat lake, six miles long and with difficult shores that usually drop off far too steeply for comfortable wading. But a road runs along one side, within a quarter of a mile of the lake for most of the way, and there are many arms and bays that one can plow around and reach in some sort of fashion by walking out on fallen trees. It is a beautiful lake, islanded and set among the hills, with tall white mountains always distantly visible. I like to fish it because of this beauty and because there are often sudden surface rises of good fish in the narrow arms of the lake. I cannot remember that I have even hooked or seen a fish bigger than sixteen inches on these rises, but the size of the lake and the abundance of feed among the rotting trees of its shoreline convince me that big fish are there somewhere. And on a sudden surface rise one day I hope to find one.

Yellowthroat Lake is tiny and round and easy. It is full of aquatic beetles, and trout come well to small dark wet flies worked among the lily pads. Yellowthroats nest every year along the swampy shoreline and I should like the lake for this alone. Goldeneye Lake has always half a dozen pairs of courting goldeneyes when I go there first in May. It has plenty of fish, Dolly Vardens and rainbows as well as cutthroats, and good shores everywhere. Its unexpected fish are the Dolly Vardens, which fight with surprising strength and are very beautiful, orange-finned, pale-spotted, with a fine-scaled brilliance of silver sheen; and the occasional fourth-year maiden cutthroats, in magnificent condition, seeming to lurk away from their fellows, attacking the fly suddenly and fiercely from the shadow of a root or the foot of a big rock along the shore.

All these lakes and many others, each with its own variation, its own special flavor of fishing, are worthy. I hold them in mind and return when I can to test and enrich the pleasure. But the lake I am looking for is another like Merit Lake. It could well be longer, with a stronger, wider stream at the head and a matching flow at the outlet. But it must have the same firm-bottomed, gently sloping shore, the same clean and silvery cutthroats, the same quiet rises at sunset.

I never think of boat or raft on Merit Lake, except at one or two soft and marshy spots where there are few fish anyway, or perhaps in the deep little bay just to the left of the stream that comes in at the head. The rest of the mile or so of shoreline can be waded easily and quietly; in many places one can work out a hundred feet or more to cover a promising rise.

If the lake is quiet, as it can be at times, one can follow the stream below the outlet as it wanders through a mile or more of swamps, now running swiftly over a rocky bed, now spreading into a pond-sized pothole or idling through a deep still reach. There is fishing of every kind in this length and trout of almost equal variety, though they are all, so far as I know, cutthroats. I have caught little black fish of three or four inches, tiny but fully mature replicas of spawning three- or four-pounders; and then, only a few feet from them a silvery pounder in perfect shape. In the miniature pools of the rocky reaches, fingerlings rise with solemn dignity that often fails to draw down a No. 10 dry fly, yet once I hooked in such a pool a broadheaded, snake-bodied black monster of eighteen inches.

That fish surprised me a little. I can understand the silvery pounders; undoubtedly they have dropped down from the lake. But I don't think the lake holds any really big fish; I don't really know why it shouldn't, except that I have never seen or risen anything that seemed bigger than the occasional sixteen-incher I have killed from it; but I think the monster grew in a pothole, on bullheads and sticklebacks and his smaller relatives. He had spawned only a month or two before he rose to my floating fly in the miniature pool, and I like to believe his pothole became a happier place for that mistake.

The big fish of Merit Lake are fourteen-, fifteen- and occasionally sixteen-inchers. They are bright, clean fish with many small black spots, and for cutthroats they are free surface risers and bold jumpers. I think of wading out at the head of the lake on a spring evening, as the west wind dies and the shadow of the hill comes over the water. Fish rise out of reach in the bay on the far side of the stream, two or three ten-inchers rise steadily in the streaky current itself. There is no hurry. Go out a little and wait quietly. Throw a fly if you like, let it sit on the water or twitch it gently. A fish rolls over it, comes again and has it. He jumps at once, bright in the fading light and runs off toward the center of the lake. A good fish rises along the shore, and another. One hurries a little, nets the hooked fish, dries the fly with quick false casts that let out line at the same time. The first rise is covered and the fly sits boldly on the gleaming water. A blue grouse, going to roost, rustles nervously in the trees behind. Hooters are still noisy on the far hills. Time to lift the fly. But stir it first, and with that he comes. So for a precious twenty or thirty minutes as the light fails, slowly and gently and quietly.

One could wish Merit Lake a wider, stronger stream, a bolder place in the hills, bigger fish. Yet I think I like it the way it is, a true little lake, a good little lake, and an early one.

The Maculate Purist

O<small>NE DOES NOT EXACTLY CHOOSE TO</small> become a purist—it is a conviction that overtakes one. Once upon a time I thought it an undesirable limitation and resolved that I should never be overtaken by it. I am still the broadest kind of a purist: I stay with the fly only, for trout and salmon fishing, but I will use anything that could reasonably be called a fly for these fish; and for other fish, from which one can expect less co-operation, I will use whatever is necessary. Even with Pacific salmon my conviction is not wholehearted and I don't mind using spoons and spinners, or even herring, in salt water, though I am not an enthusiast.

I have believed for a long time that all fresh-water trout, except for a few surly and unimportant monsters down on the murky beds of deep lakes, can and should be caught on the fly. I have no special objection to proving a point or testing a theory by using a spinner or lure, but a departure of this kind must be only a minor interlude. If I am going fishing simply for the pleasure of fishing I will catch my trout on the fly or do without one. The use of a fly is every bit as essential to the sport as the use of a rod. I will not limit myself to dry fly, even for fresh-water trout, because I believe that both wet and dry flies have their uses and their fascination. But I'm inclined to think it is a waste of pleasure to catch fish on a sunk fly when they could be taken on a floater.

It is only within the last five years that I have rigidly abstained from fishing for steelhead with anything but the fly. I still have nothing against the use of spinners and other artificial lures, at least for winter fish, but I avoid them simply because they are generally more effective than any techniques I have been able to develop with the fly. To use them at all is to be tempted to use them far too much; so much, in fact, that one never gives the fly a real chance to prove itself and never gives oneself a sufficient incentive to learn how to use the fly effectively.

I am quite satisfied now that any good fisherman can get himself a fair share of winter steelhead on the fly, and have a much more interesting time doing it than he would have in catching more fish by some other means. I also believe that if more fishermen would devote themselves exclusively to the fly in winter they would soon develop better techniques than any I have been able to think up.

One fish I have not yet been able to catch on the fly is the big spring, chinook or tyee salmon. I know he can be caught on spoons, plugs and spinners of all kinds in fresh water, and I can't see a reason in the world why he should not be fooled into grabbing at some form of fly at least once in a while. Since the big fall-running fish are only in the river for two or three weeks before they begin to deteriorate, opportunity for experiment is limited; unless I keep faithfully plugging flies at their heads whenever I have thè chance to, I feel I shall never know the answer; so I keep to flies except for the occasional use of a spinner after a pool has been thoroughly worked over with a fly, to satisfy myself that the fish can be moved.

All this adds up to a fairly confused picture, but it seems to be the picture of a sufficiently obstinate purist, at least by western standards. I can think of no reason against being a purist; it is strictly a matter of individual preference, and even purists like Halford, to whom anything but the dry fly was sin, have a right to their preference. But at the same time I often wonder why anyone as lazy, as fond of fishing and so little concerned with dogma as myself should have chosen such a hard path.

The truth is that I have been led to it by several converging lines of thought or feeling. It is true that I am lazy, and for that reason the simplicity and compactness of fly-fishing tackle has a great appeal for me; I long ago became thoroughly scared of the ramifications of other tackle—the mass of baits and lures and hooks one acquires, the problem of carrying two outfits up the river so as to be able to change to something else if the fly did not take fish; or the mental conflict of deciding, before starting out, whether the day suggested fly rod or casting rod. Neither sport nor art should be unnecessarily cluttered and complicated, so a wise man, once he is satisfied that the fish he is after will respond to a fly, is almost bound to be convinced by the clean simplicity of the gear alone.

Out of this simplicity of gear, the light and graceful rod, smooth line, uncomplicated reel, the gut balanced to the fish and the single hook whose whole deceit is merely a matter of hair and feathers, grows the sport's keenest satisfaction. Only hand and arm and eye can draw performance from the combination, and it can be performance of infinite grace and subtlety. Even without the help of the fish it is an absorbing business; when the fish does respond the elegance of the performance is continued, both in the manner of the response, which is clear and clean and usually visible, and in everything that follows, which is unhampered by such things as leads and swivels, multiple hooks and odd pieces of wood or metal. After some thirty years of fishing, during which I have tried most methods, I am satisfied that to catch a fish which might have been caught on the fly, in any other way is a waste of fish, a waste of sport and denial of a high experience. If a trout doesn't want my flies he can stay in his river to provide sport for a better fly-fisherman or a bite to eat for the hardware operator.

All this is opinion, of course, and largely emotional. But I believe that if one can catch fish on a fly one owes it to one's fellow anglers to do so; and if one cannot there is just as strong an obligation to learn how. As has often before been noticed, a fly-fisherman can work over a stream in such a way as to leave it practically undisturbed for the next man. He can also in large measure select his fish. And he can return unharmed any fish he does not want. These are things of enormous importance on heavily fished public waters, which is what most of the waters of North America are. They spread the sport much farther than it could otherwise go and they could, by themselves, insure the future of many streams and lakes that are being rapidly fished out by bait and hardware.

So I'll stay with the fly from now on. I haven't so many fish left to catch that I can afford to settle for the lesser pleasure. A time will come all too soon when I shall only be fit to troll a spoon over the stern of a boat or dabble a worm from a wheel chair.

The Unexpected Fish

INEVITABLY THERE IS GREAT SATISFAC-
tion in catching the exact fish one is fishing for; a big
fish of his kind, yet not extravagantly big, rising or
lying precisely where he should be, coming to the fly
confidently and smoothly, fighting with anticipated
vigor, sliding at last to net or gaff or beach in the calculated place. This is the reward of experience and performance, good to watch and good to achieve. Pre-

sumably it is the principal objective of going fishing. Yet the fish one remembers are not these noble creatures of orthodoxy and perfection but the unexpected fish, the almost impossible fish, that catch one with tackle and body off balance, and force improvisation and shocked, stumbling, cross-legged incompetence.

It is impossible to create such fish deliberately, by going out with inadequate tackle for instance, because their essence is to be unexpected. The closest one can come to it is to go out and fish calmly and conscientiously for fifteen- or sixteen-inch trout in a stream that also has a run of big steelhead or Atlantic salmon; but even this fails after two or three times, because experience steps in and makes the unexpected more than half-expected. One cannot do it with steelhead kelts in a spring trout stream, with a giant halibut or ling cod when looking for salmon or with an oversize Dolly Varden in a lake of small trout, because these are all pretty much undesirables and it is essential that the unexpected fish be very much desired. There is no harm in hoping, in an offhand way, for an unexpected fish, but any too precise optimism will destroy him in advance by making him expected.

One unexpected fish that leaves me a little cold is the great, unyielding brute who takes a wet fly on 2 or 3x gut when it is at fullest stretch downstream, just as one starts to recover line; about all he adds up to is a solid pull, a lost fly and a moment of annoyance; one hasn't even time to blame oneself for heavy-handedness. His broad-backed brother, who shoulders suddenly out of a fast little run where a two-pounder should have been lying and seems to break 4x gut against the friction of the line on the water, is almost as bad. There is a limited hope that either fish may come again, but usually one can only mark the place and season for future caution. To resolve upon perpetual caution, a constant delicate anticipation of the unexpected, is to interfere too much with the easy pleasure of fishing though the shades of the mentors of one's youth will try to argue that this should be the lesson learned.

The first August steelhead I ever caught in the Campbell was the ideal of the unexpected fish. I was working a No. 6 Silver Brown with a 2x leader on a long slow swing across the tail of the Canyon Pool, expecting nothing more than a three- or four-pound cutthroat, secured in the expectation by the experience of six or eight seasons. The big fish took midway on the swing right at the surface, with a slash that sent a spout of water several inches into the air above the smooth pool. I let the drag of the line strike him and he ran upstream from the pull, keeping well to the middle, away from all trouble, wearing down his first surge of strength and giving me time to realize what it was all about. He could have broken me at any time during the first ten minutes and would have been well within his rights in doing so. After that he was under the control of the rod, though still dangerously heavy and strong. If he had flipped over and broken the gut as I beached him I should probably not have blamed myself much. He did not, and he weighed sixteen pounds.

I caught three or four more August and September steelheads of ten or twelve pounds in seasons after that before I realized that the river had a small late run of big summer fish. They are no longer altogether unexpected, but the run is too sparse for one to go out and deliberately fish for them. It is a time to look for two- or three-pound trout, with appropriate tackle, so the big fish retain many of the exciting qualities of the unexpected.

A fish need not be extremely large to qualify in the unexpected class. I shall remember a brown trout of my boyhood, not over a pound in weight, which escaped into a weed bed and broke me. He stayed where he was, head burrowed into the weeds and only an inch or two of his back showing intermittently as the long green strands moved in the current over it. I waded cautiously toward him from downstream, the net ready in my hand, though I hadn't any very clear idea of what I intended to do; I had tried and failed before to net trout out of weed beds. When I was still six or eight feet below him he came suddenly to life, darted out of the weed bed and a little way upstream. For a moment he rested there uncertainly, then turned and came downstream for his holt like a bullet. I thrust the net toward the line of his flight in a forlorn reflex action and felt a surge of astonished triumph as he thudded into it. He was my fish all right, with my little ginger quill trailing broken 4x gut from his mouth.

Last winter was cold, so cold that I shouldn't write of it in a book of springtime fishing. Towards the end of January I finished a book and felt I had to go fishing, though the weather was around zero and there was four feet of snow on the ground. Ann told me to be sure and get a fish because it was a long while since we had had one. I knew I shouldn't be fishing long in any sort of comfort, so I waded in a few yards above a good lie and began to work my fly out over it as quickly as possible. A fine fish took the fly almost at once, well out in the fast water, and ran strongly seventy or eighty yards downstream. There was ice in the rings of the rod already and when the wet backing began to come in I saw that it was coated with ice, so I began to worry a little and handle the fish carefully. The splice between backing and fly line jammed in the ice of the top ring, but I broke it through and felt a fine sense of relief when it came on to the reel. He took it out again twice and caused me plenty of other trouble and anxiety, but I had him at last within reach of the gaff and fairly quiet. I was standing among large boulders, in two or three feet of moderate current, but I knew I had to gaff him there because I dared not take him nearer the ice at the edge of the river.

I was standing awkwardly and the fish was lying awkwardly, head a little down and still upright. I judged him about fifteen pounds and thought several things one has no business to think when about to gaff a fish. I thought: that hook's got a light hold. If I try to shift him he'll run again and he might shake the hook or even get into the ice along the shore. I want him very much, because it's going to be tough fishing from here on, with ice just about solid in the rings and on the line, and forming faster than you can break it loose. With him on the bank it won't matter much—at least I can relax and enjoy myself. . . . So I reached the gaff back-handedly over him and made the stroke. It was a bad one, too far forward and not solid, but it pierced the gill cover and I lifted the fish, swung him across and started towards the bank, holding him out of the water on the gaff. As I made the first step, the point of the gaff broke off and the fish fell back into the water. I saw the gut was wrapped around the broken hook of the gaff.

For one quick moment as I tried to free the gut, the fish was quiet. Then he gulped water and expelled a cloud of blood from his gills, turned and ran. I made one last move to free the gut, then it broke and he was gone.

In spite of my successive stupidities, I managed to feel quite sorry for myself, and at the same time disgusted. I knew from that cloud of blood I had killed the fish—fish don't have much blood to lose. So he was wasted. And the chance of another with the freezing line that would no longer shoot a yard was pretty small.

Out of my shame, in an unpromising attempt to reduce it a little, I developed the idea that I might find the fish if he died quickly. The river was quite low and for a hundred yards or more below me the current set slightly towards the bank, running at an uneven three to five feet among big boulders. I started fishing again, but watched the water below me.

After about five minutes of fishing I saw a faint white reflection in the water a few feet below where my fly was working. I lost it, then saw it again. It was far too easy to account for—the white rock, I told myself, in the lower lie. But I kept watching, and after a while it showed again, thirty or forty feet farther downstream. I admitted it was too far out to do me any good, but fished on a little faster and still kept watching. It disappeared, showed again, disappeared again. I was casting in a sort of a way, but paying no attention to the fly and hurrying over the big round boulders in a way that threatened to put me off my feet at any moment. Then the flash showed again, still farther down but close to water that might not be over my waders. I knew it was my fish now, because I had seen the twisting shape of his body as he came up through the water, and I knew it was my last hope, because the current set out again just below where he was. I reeled up and hurried.

When I got to where he should have been there was no sign of him. I didn't want to be too hopeful, because the whole affair seemed moderately unlikely, but at the same time I was quite determined to stay with the fish as long as there was any hope at all.

He showed suddenly, starting from the bottom belly up in a twisting effort that carried him almost to the surface, a few feet out from me and a few feet below. Then he sank slowly back and disappeared. I waded out and down, on tiptoe in the current, with an occasional flick of ice water slopping over the waders against my chest. I peered down into the water and saw the fish, right side up, curved against the upstream side of a rock, held against it by the current. Then I remembered the point of the gaff was broken off. I thought of lowering my fly down on the tip of my rod, decided against it and pushed the broken gaff towards him. It meant putting my arm in up to the shoulder but I reached him, got the remains of the hook well under him, and heaved. It didn't go home, but he came up on it almost to the surface, then slipped off. I raked the broken gaff along the length of him, hoping it might catch in the gills. It did. I lifted his head clear of the water, set my fingers in his gills and waded ashore. He weighed fourteen pounds, which is not large for a winter fish, and any triumph I could claim was born of clumsiness and poor judgment. But he rates high among my unexpected fish.

If doing the wrong thing can make an unexpected fish, it is far more certain that an unexpected fish can make one do the wrong thing. Not so long ago I was standing under April sunshine in a shallow, sandy slough at the head of a big lake. There were trout in the slough, handsome green-backed cutthroats up to two pounds or so, but they weren't moving much at that time of day. So I was wading cautiously along, hoping to see one against the pale sand. I was watching the edges of the slough mostly, expecting the fish to be close under the matted tangle of swamp brush that hung down into the water, so I did not see the big fish until he was almost opposite me.

He was swimming majestically, calmly, very slowly, right up the center of the slough. He was broad and deep and long, and I will say he weighed seven pounds, though I am quite sure he weighed over ten pounds. I have never knowingly put a fly over a cutthroat even nearly so big.

55

He passed me without a tremor of his fins to suggest he had seen me and I remained for a long moment in frozen hesitation. I thought of only two things: that I was going to put a fly over him and that I mustn't move to do so until he was far enough away. I did not manage to remember that I was fishing a No. 14 variant on 4x gut in my search for two-pounders, nor that the big fish was now trapped between me and the head of the slough, so that I could easily take time to change my rigging on the certainty I would find him again. I simply waited until his lazy swimming had carried him ten or twelve yards beyond me, then began to put out line in cautious but rapid false casts.

He was about sixty feet away when I gave it to him. I had the sense to set the fly to one side and a little ahead of him and the luck to make a shepherd's crook that kept the gut farther from him than the fly. As a cast, it was a pretty smooth operation all through—at one moment the flat, calm surface of the slough was empty, in the next my fly was there without a ripple to show how it had arrived. The big trout saw it and turned instantly towards it, probably wondering how the nymph had passed up through the water without being seen. There was no change of pace, only of direction. Very slowly he came, nudged the fly with his nose, took it down. I tightened on him and thought I was quite a fisherman.

Right in the second the little fly hit him, the fish knew he had no business in the slough and I began to suspect I had no business being hooked up to him. He was past me, trailing slack line, before I could turn around, and the line was tight again and the reel running before I could begin stumbling after him. Just for a moment he kept to the open slough and I kidded myself I still had a chance. Then the drag of the reel worried him and he cut over among the drowned tips of the swamp brush. The reel ran out a few more yards and stopped. I saw the flash of a broad, bright side in the brush, a splash and that was the end of it. I felt very lonely.

If they ever come to writing life insurance under water, the unexpected fish will be a pretty good risk. But I'd rather lose one honest example of the type than land a hundred orthodox creatures. It's nice to be reminded that one cannot put a line in the water without tempting the unknown.

Recognizing Birds

MOST FISHERMEN ARE INTERESTED in birds and enjoy seeing them when they are out fishing. But a surprising number of men who have fished for years cannot put names to some of the commonest birds they see; usually they are apologetic and regretful about this, but they seem resigned to it, as though recognizing birds and naming them were some obscure art, not open to everyone.

To some extent I think the ornithologists have been responsible for this. Like most scientists they have been, quite properly, introverted and specialized, deeply concerned with tiny differences and an infinity of subspecies. Unwilling to trust to impressions, they have described birds minutely, from vast collections of skins, with a confusion of distinguishing detail that the ordinary observer has no chance to see. Most of us who have any interest at all in outdoor life have known the frustration of trying to name what we have seen from such descriptions, and I can only think that many men I have known have given up altogether after the first few attempts. I know my own enthusiasm has been checked time and again.

Any long-term countryman, gunner or woodsman knows many birds almost as a matter of habit, whether or not he can put the right names to them or describe the precise means he uses for recognition. This is identification by experience, through repeated casual observation; it is also probably the best and surest identification there is, except that it deals only with major differences and it is a fairly slow process. To speed it up and make it more generally useful, one has to analyze it and learn to apply the component parts consciously.

The principal means of identification are voice, color, shape and movement, in reverse order of usefulness and importance. I have a dull ear and don't trust it especially, but I use it often enough to tell mallard from wigeon, song sparrow from robin, crow from raven, or one goose from another; so a man with a good ear could well find it very useful indeed. Color is a treacherous thing, often difficult or impossible to see and varying markedly in different lights. But under the right conditions it can be an easy means of recognition and there are times when nothing else will do. Shape, in which I suppose one may fairly include size, is a faithful thing, nearly always visible and reliable. Movement is a whole story, or rather a multitude of stories. Speed of wing-beat will tell pigeon from crow almost as far as the eye can see; the leaping rise of a mallard from the water is as distinctive as his green head under most conditions; the dipping of a water ouzel, the sleek dive of a loon, the level-winged sailing of an eagle are all distinctive things; and if hawks and flycatchers and hummingbirds all hover, they do so very differently.

To move these obvious factors, which everyone uses, up into the field of conscious observation is the first and only really important step one has to make toward getting informed pleasure out of birds. The easiest way to make it is to be a child under the guidance of some fairly impatient adult whose good opinion one cares for; failing this one just has to want to know one bird from another and be content to apply the mind a little. Fortunately there has at last arisen an ornithologist who is both willing and able to help the ordinary observer to identification by exactly these means that eye and mind use most easily and naturally. Roger Tory Peterson's *Field Guides* to the birds of North America are the sort of books that anyone can use with profit and complete faith. The work of putting these books together must have been enormous, but I can't think of any more worthwhile service that has ever been done for the man who likes to use his eyes to some purpose when he is wandering along beside a stream or through the bush.

It may seem strange to write of birds so directly in

a fishing book. But I can think of no book that pretends to describe the pleasures of fishing without some reference to birds. Dame Juliana gives a careful list of the waterside birds that add to the angler's pleasure, and all the later enthusiasts pay their tribute, small or large. Some, such as Grey of Fallodon, might have been hard put to it to say whether birds or fish contributed more to the pleasure of any day's fishing, and there are very few of us who will not neglect our own fishing to watch an osprey or a heron at his, or to admire the plumage and display of a drake merganser or goldeneye in the breeding season.

It would be carrying the thing much too far to suggest that every angler owes it to his sport to become an ornithologist. But it seems clear that a man is missing something if he does not know the drumming of a ruffed grouse from the hoot of a blue grouse, if he cannot tell an eagle from an osprey or a merganser from a goldeneye. I have fished with men to whom these distinctions and many others were like a language from another world, but I have never fished with one who did not want them explained or who did not continue on his own to other discoveries once they had been explained.

There really is nothing difficult or obscure about recognizing birds and knowing something of them. Rather, it is a rapid and cumulative process. Inevitably one starts out with some knowledge—very few fishermen cannot recognize such birds as kingfishers and herons, swallows, jays, robins and a few others. Everyone knows a duck from a hawk or an eagle from a sparrow, and it is not hard to guess that a bird pounding his beak on a dead tree is some kind of woodpecker. From there on it is only a matter of two or three seasons of conscious interest to identify all the birds one commonly sees on any given stretch of fishing water; and that is enough to make other identifications almost easy.

Perhaps I have said too much about identifications. The pleasure, after all, is in watching, not in calling names. The big duck with the narrow scarlet beak, the handsome dark green head, dark back and white flanks, kicking up little spurts of water with brilliant orange feet for the admiration of his gray-backed, red-headed female, is not less beautiful because he is nameless. The big bird that hunts over the water on wide, curving wings and sweeps or plunges in long-legged dives to pick up small fish is no less impressive without a name. Yet it is worth knowing he is an osprey, just as it is worth knowing that the drab little duck with the white eye spots, warily keeping its distance off a stream mouth in a summer lake, is a female harlequin, probably with a nest not far away. If one does know, it is easy to go to a book and learn more of the bird, easy to share the experience with someone else and perhaps gain more from that.

Birds share a fisherman's world and are part of his scene. Many are themselves fishermen. They are beauty and interest and associations, and they grow richer in meaning with every recognition, every added observation. It is possible, I suppose, to disregard them and still be a fisherman. But to do so is to miss the sport's most brilliant counterpoint.

Putting Fish Back

I DECIDED TO WONDER THE OTHER DAY just how many fish a year I kill to make my sport. So I looked back over the records, missing out most of the war years and stopping short of those years when I was working hard to try and learn about fish—how they grow, when they spawn, what they feed on, why they are fat or lean or dark or light. The answer seems to be, from ten to twenty steelheads, summer and winter; about a dozen salmon, a little less than fifty cutthroat and rainbow trout.

These are not big figures. I knew a man who used to kill every year over a thousand trout in two months' fishing on a big lake; later in the year he used to kill around three hundred salmon, sometimes in catches of thirty or forty in a single day. He always fished from a boat, always with a fly, usually with two rods. And he liked to kill fish. I think he was nuts; he thought I was nuts. If the point of going fishing is to catch and kill fish, undoubtedly he was right. If the point of going fishing is to have a good time with a minimum of destruction, maybe I have a point.

Even so, my figures are probably larger than they need be. Having a wife and four children who like to eat fish, I undoubtedly kill a few each year that might otherwise have been turned back. And I still occasionally kill a fish because I want to learn something about him that I do not think I can learn in any other way.

It is reasonable to ask at this point: why such reluctance in a professed fisherman to kill fish? The main reason, I suppose, is that I don't enjoy killing anything, so I cannot see that doing so adds to the sport of going fishing. But I also have the feeling that there are not and cannot be enough fish of the kinds I am mainly interested in to go around the steadily increasing numbers of anglers. I know there are places where trout are so numerous that a heavy intensity of fishing is needed to keep them at a worthwhile size and prevent deterioration of their food resources; but I do not often fish such places, and if I did so I should feel reasonably certain that there would be plenty of other fishermen all too willing to apply the necessary pressure.

Really worthwhile fish, like migratory cutthroats and rainbows, Atlantic salmon, Pacific salmon and non-migratory trout of good size, are nowhere so numerous that they threaten their own future. They are nowhere sufficiently numerous to withstand unlimited fishing. And only rarely—never in waters easily accessible by road—are they able to hold their own against the determination of anglers to kill them, and of industry to poison them or bar them out or dry up their water supply. If one is convinced of this, as I am, some thought of limiting one's own killing is inevitable.

The first and most obvious limitation is by method—limiting oneself to artificial lures only or to fly only or to particularly fine tackle—and from this there is an immediate gain in improved sport. But it does not go far enough; fly only, even dry fly only, in the right hands and under the right conditions can kill a lot of fish, as my fly-fishing friend showed when he counted his trout by thousands and his salmon by hundreds. Nor are the legal limits set on anglers by states and provinces even nearly good enough, as is clearly shown by their periodic downward revision as fishing intensity increases and the yields of sport grow slim. I have seen the British Columbia bag limit of trout reduced from twenty-four to fifteen to twelve within the space of twenty years, and I shall undoubtedly see it reduced still further. And almost as surely, good fishing within the reduced limits will become harder and harder to find.

I think the wise fisherman, who knows what is good for the present and future of his sport, usually pays little attention to the size limits or the bag limits allowed by most game commissions. Six, or at most eight inches, is the usual minimum size limit for trout. But I have yet to see a six- or eight-inch trout that was worth a sportman's while, except to fill an immediate, frying-pan need; even nine- and ten-inch trout are pathetically small fish and I'm inclined to think that from a fisher-man's point of view a trout hardly becomes a trout until it is at least ten inches long; below that size it is a creature of promise, not fulfillment.

I find I develop rather quickly a clear idea of what kind of trout I want from almost any water. Usually I can say I don't want anything smaller than twelve inches, and stay faithfully enough to that. Occasionally I settle for ten; more often fourteen seems about right. There is a sort of relationship here between size and numbers; roughly, I should say, twelve ten-inch trout make a good bag, or eight twelve-inchers, or six four-teen-inch fish. Which doesn't mean one has to go all out to kill such limits or must necessarily stop at them if they are below legal limits; simply that they are good controls to keep in mind. As often as not a brace of fourteen- or sixteen-inch fish are plenty to bring home; occasionally, for some special purpose, one may need a few more. But to kill a legal limit of fish every time it is possible to do so seems to me the height of folly and waste.

There are other ways of setting one's own limits. I shall never again kill three winter steelhead in one day, for instance, because I think that is too many, even though the law allows it. Two is a better limit and one is all I usually bring home. One coho salmon is all I ever want from a stream in a day's fishing—if the fish happen to be taking well it is quite easy to turn them loose. Half a dozen sea-run cutthroats are enough for me or any other man in one day; estuary fish are too accessible for common sense to permit more killing than that.

I fish a good deal in one big lake that has seven tribu-tary streams, all of which are good. Most of the streams are widely separated, and by rowboat it is a minor feat to fish more than two or three of them in a single day. With an outboard one can reach them all and fish them all within twelve or fourteen hours, and occasionally it is pleasant to do so. But there is an obvious obligation to recognize the improved transportation by some sort of limit. The one I have found most interesting is a limit of not more than one fish from each creek, the fish to be not less than fourteen inches and taken on a floating fly. It is not an easy limit to achieve, because one is almost certain to find at least one creek where the fish are determinedly off their feeding. And it is a limit that is certainly not going to harm anything if it is achieved.

But all bag limits are evil if they are regarded as a mark to fish for or shoot at, and this is almost invariably what happens to them. They are set as control, as a maximum not to be exceeded. Instead of using them in this way the hunter or fisherman tends to use them as a minimum measure of his sport; "I got my limit in a couple of hours," he will say. Or, if things didn't work out that well he will come home almost ashamed to admit that his skill has not yielded him every last measure of death the law allows, regardless of whether his day has been a good one. I have two hopes for the future. The first and lesser one is that game commissions will one day have sense enough to set limits that measurably reflect the sport safely available. The second and deeply urgent one is that we shall grow a race of sportsmen no one of whom will ever consider it a matter for pride to have killed a limit.

The fisherman's enormous advantage in the matter of bag limits is that he can limit his killing without appreciably limiting his sport, and he can also select what he does kill in a way that is seldom possible in other sports. True, the big game hunter can select for head or size with care; the duck hunter can wait for certain species and limit himself to drakes only. But once the shot is fired the choice is made and there is no release from it for hunter or hunted. The fisherman can throw his fly, rise and hook and play his fish, even net him or beach him or hold him in his hands—and still return him un-harmed to life.

It is often claimed that it is difficult to return a fish safely to the water. I am satisfied that it is not. A little knowledge is necessary, a little understanding of how a fish works, and a few reasonably precise and confident hand movements. Fish that have been netted will not die, as some people believe, "because the mesh has cut the slime and exposed the fish to disease." Fish handled with dry hands will not die from this alone. Fish dropped back into the water from a reasonable height will not die. These are tales spread by men who want an excuse for killing all the fish they catch, and experience simply does not bear them out.

As a generalization, it is safe to say that the smaller a fish is, the easier it is to give him his freedom. He will not exhaust himself so much as a larger fish, the hook frees more readily from his softer mouth, and his smaller body seems to react more promptly to renewed flow of water through his gills. It is also true that while a fly-fisherman should be able to release safely very nearly a hundred per cent of the fish he hooks, a bait fisherman cannot hope to do nearly so well because of the tendency of the fish to take the bait farther down into their throats.

One of the most important rules in releasing fish is to do so with a minimum of handling. I have released hundreds of fish, including salmon and steelhead, without ever taking them out of the water—simply by reaching down, gripping the shank of the hook and twisting it out. This is hard on the fly, but never on the fish. When a fish must be handled, it is best to hold him by the tail or lower jaw if possible, and still without taking him out of the water. But I have freed many good-sized trout by netting them, lifting them out of the net by the lower jaw, freeing the hook with my other hand, then putting them gently back in the water, using an easy hold on tail or body with the second hand only after they are in the water.

The danger in handling fish is not, it seems, in the warmth or dryness of the hand, but in exerting pressure that damages vital organs. Some years ago I read of an experiment that tested the relative safety of handling fish with wet or dry hands. Of large numbers of fish handled in both ways, the percentage survival of those handled with dry hands was considerably greater, and the conclusion was that the greater pressure necessary to hold fish in wet hands had damaged vital organs and so caused the higher mortality. That is why I feel sure a minimum of handling is desirable and why I believe that pressure, when necessary, is best applied at the wrist of the tail, on the back or on the lower jaw.

A fish that has lost a considerable amount of blood probably will not survive; fish have small hearts and the blood circulates slowly and at low pressure, so there is not much blood to be lost. A fish that cannot hold itself upright and swim away probably will not survive, especially if it is a large fish. Large fish like steelheads and salmon must often be completely exhausted

68

before they can be beached and freed from the hook. To give them a chance it is essential to hold them upright in the stream while they gulp some water through their gills and regain enough oxygen to strengthen themselves. If they are slow to do this, it pays to draw them gently back and forth through the water to start the gills moving. Usually they will swim away after less than a minute of this treatment, but I have released them and grabbed them again to continue the treatment when they seemed unable to hold an even keel. I have never found again a fish that swam strongly away from me; I don't think I have ever failed to find again one that could not regain enough strength to hold itself upright, though I have sometimes left them in sheltered water in the hope they would recover.

The test of the survival of fish that have been handled is in the return of the thousands upon thousands of fish that have been marked or tagged. And any fisherman who wants to convince himself of the recuperative powers of fish has only to remember those he has caught with the healed scars of formidable wounds. I have caught healed and healthy fish whose eyes or jaws or both had been torn away by hooks, fish whose whole bodies were deeply net-scarred, fish so deeply bitten by seals and other predators that they seemed deformed. The prick of a hook, a few minutes of dancing on the end of a line, the gentle handling of skillful release, will not kill creatures designed to survive the batterings of a dangerous lifetime.

Local Knowledge

T HERE IS NO SUBSTITUTE FOR SOUND local knowledge. Long and wide experience is the next best thing, but it can rarely produce the same results as quickly and it will inevitably overlook many of the little chancy things that build up local knowledge—the discovery of a lie in unpromising water between two good pools, the presence of an unusual run of fish in a certain place at a certain season, the influence of tide in estuaries, the timing of local hatches of feed, and so on.

But sound local knowledge is a rare thing, or at best

hard to find. And unsound local knowledge, usually readily accessible, has probably done more to deprive good anglers of the fruits their unfettered experience might have yielded than any other one cause. It usually takes a negative form; the local fish won't take a fly, they can't be caught in fresh water, they won't do this, they won't do that. Very occasionally such negative information may be sound. But far more often it is pure myth, of uncertain origin, and only the lethargy of the local fishermen has kept it sacred. It can go well beyond a small locality, too; in fact it can blanket the coast of a whole continent. Even today a majority of Pacific Coast fishermen still believe that winter steelhead won't take a fly, and large numbers of them believe they will move only for salmon eggs. I know one Vancouver Island stream whose locals insist that their special breed of steelheads will take only salmon eggs, even though they know that fish are consistently caught by other means in streams twenty or thirty miles away. I remember, too, the repeated warnings I used to listen to that Pacific salmon will never take anything once they have left salt water. That was a myth of twenty-five years ago, shattered a thousand times before and since, but I haven't the least doubt that it can still be found in venerated persistence here and there.

There is one good way of dealing with those negative forms of local knowledge. If they conflict with personal experience, if they seem to insult probability, don't believe them. Go ahead and try the impossible, and let the natives smile their knowing pity.

We have most of us, I suppose, had a share in creating

similar restraining myths. I can think of times and places where I have warned good fishermen not to bother with floating flies, then later, under identical conditions and in the same place, turned from wet to dry myself with excellent results. I can remember saying, "There's nothing much in the river this time of year"—only to go out in the same week of the same month in a later year and find the fish there.

It's bad enough when the unhappy visitor has to hunt his way among all these complications of local mis-knowledge. But the most insidious and deadly form is the one that a man builds up inside himself, to fool himself. It usually grows out of habit and laziness and improperly assessed experience. Not that any of these easygoing attributes is a vice or in any way to be condemned; a fisherman has every right to be lazy and a creature of habit and a poor logician. But they can interfere with catching fish.

One of the commonest tricks of self-deception is to fish over a likely-looking stretch of water once or twice without result and then, having found fish above it and below it, call it no good and pass it up. Because I enjoy more than almost anything else in fishing the discovery of a new lie in water I believe I know thoroughly, I try quite hard not to fall into this trap. But I do fall into it, and I tempt others into it. Even more easily, I fall into the belief that I know the runs of a migratory stream and their seasons. A few sharp surprises, one of them last year in a river I have fished regularly through more than fifteen seasons, have persuaded me to be much more cautious about accepting my own experience of migratory runs. Either one can completely overlook a run while fishing all around it year after year, or a new and important run can develop suddenly where there had previously been nothing of the sort. I am inclined to believe the second possibility is the more likely of the two.

It may not be worth questioning local opinion on such points as these, but if previous experience, in the form of a pressing hunch, suggests that local knowledge may be at fault, it is a good idea to give the hunch a chance. So far as I am concerned, good-looking water is good water, until I have proved it otherwise. And I have a firm mental resolve to remember that good-looking water on a stream I fish frequently remains potentially good and at least worth an occasional check unless I find some clear-cut explanation for its failure to produce. There is one pool on the Campbell where I have never moved a fish of any kind nor, so far as I know, has anyone else; but I can't see a reason in the world why it shouldn't hold fish, so I put a fly through it from time to time—not as often as I should but often enough, I hope, to prove my original hunch before I die.

When all this has been said, local knowledge remains just about the only short cut to good fishing in most places. No amount of experience will reveal all the secrets of a stream in a day or two; and while one may hit the fish luckily on a first visit to new water, there will always be something hidden that local knowledge could have made plain. The boy with the can of worms has seen fish and probably caught them in half a dozen spots where the surface of the water gives no reason to expect them.

Guides are paid to have sound local knowledge and the best of them have it. But the best of them can be wrong and plenty know very little more than how to get to the water one wants to fish. But I am not thinking of professional guides at the moment. In many places there are none, and most fishermen who work from their feet rather than from boats don't use professional guides. Local knowledge is everywhere, in the hotel or resort owner, in the postmaster and the garageman and the liquor vendor, in the brother angler met by the waterside and the schoolboy walking the dusty road. I once fished a long and lovely stream, looking for summer steelhead that I believed must be there. I asked everybody I met about the fish and no one had a suggestion to offer until a truck driver stopped on a bridge to watch me. When I told him what I was looking for he glanced quickly at his watch.

"Jump in the truck," he said. "I haven't been up there this year, but it's the right time for them to be around."

He drove me five or six miles, turning and twisting along overgrown side roads, and we came at last to the river again, far above where I had been fishing. I looked downstream towards a series of promising pools, but he shook his head and pointed to the wide, even sweep of water upstream. "That's where they'll be," he said, and led me through the brush to the head of the sweep. I looked at the water, wondering where and how to begin. It was a moderate current, apparently of even three- or four-foot depth from bank to bank over a bottom of gravel and sandstone. I could not see the break of a rock or snag or other protection anywhere in it.

"Wade straight out about a dozen paces," he told me. "Throw your fly another thirty feet or so and let it come round."

I did as he said and a five-pounder took my first cast. It ran ten or fifteen yards, jumped twice and the hook came free. I took in the line. "Twenty feet further out," the truck driver said. "And a little upstream."

I made the cast and fished it blank. "A little more upstream," he said, and I cast again and hooked a fish. The hook held it this time and I waded out with the fish.

"Look," I said. "How do you know where they are as close as that?"

He pointed across the river to a heavy-branched maple that leaned far out over the water. "See that tree? I used to spend hours in it every summer when I was a kid, just watching them. They're always here this time of year, lying wherever there's a little hollow scooped out of the sandstone. It's the only place they do lie, far as I know."

"Do you fish much?" I asked.

He shook his head. "Not since I was a kid. Never did go for it much. But I sure like to watch from a good place on a nice day. It's best when the salmon are running, but I always had a feeling for this place early on, like now."

He had to go then, but he showed me other lies in

the long, smooth stretch and I found fish all through it. And later, he showed me other fish, in other parts of the river, at other seasons. His was the clearest, simplest, most thorough and accurate local knowledge I have ever known. He had many observation points and no theories. His eyes were good, the clear water of his river helped him, and some interest he never fully explained gave him infinite patience. If the story has a moral it is that fishermen can afford to watch as well as to fish.

The Fish by the Cedar Stump

THE CEDAR STUMP POOL IN THE LITTLE river is a fine place to look for a steelhead in the winter, if you can get there. But that part of the river is a fifteen-mile drive over old logging grades from any traveled highway, and a foot or so of snow is enough to make it impassable; so in most winters the fish rest there peacefully, without the problem of deciding whether my flies should be intercepted or left alone.

By mid-March the snow is usually gone, or at least rotted down enough to give a car a reasonable chance. There may be a few alders and willows to clear out of the way or a wet spot to be filled in with cedar branches, but I like the pool and the other pools near it for a mile or so up- and downstream well enough to go in and look for the tail end of the winter run. In some years there are enough clean fish to make wonderful fishing; in others one releases everything that takes hold as too dark or too near spawning to be worth keeping. But that doesn't mean that the trip and its complications are not worthwhile.

The little river averages no more than fifty feet wide up here among the falls and sandstone ledges, so I take the ten-foot rod and hope the fish will not be too rough with me. In the big pool at the foot of the lower falls they usually are not. In the pool by the bridge, where they can run at once for the bad water at the head of the lower falls, I can rarely hold them. In the long series of pools below the upper falls a little effort and determination usually wins out. In the Cedar Stump Pool, which is two or three hundred yards above the bridge pool, anything can happen.

It is a long, narrow pool, fast and quite deep. In normal March water, which is fairly high, one can wade the fast water under the left bank, but it is not too comfortable. The fish usually take opposite the big cedar stump, about two-thirds of the way down the pool, where the main current spreads and slackens a little, but only a little. The tail of the pool is short and still fast, tumbling over into a short broken rapid that twists awkwardly down through thirty or forty yards to a long, wide, shallow reach.

I got through to the falls reach in mid-March for the first time this year. There was still snow on the ground, but it was soft and rotten; the weather was almost mild, the stream at a good height and clear. A fish took me rather promptly in the pool by the bridge and was friendly enough to swim back up from the tail when I slacked line on him. For a foolish moment I thought I had a chance with him, then he got nervous and ran down fast under the bridge into the bad water above the falls. He jumped twice there and was free—fortunately he threw the hook, so I still had the fly. I judged him at about twelve pounds and he seemed very bright when he jumped, so I was encouraged.

I passed the Cedar Stump Pool on the way up, walking the top of the burned-off ridge and looking down into it, but seeing nothing, as always; the water is nowhere slack enough or shallow enough in the body of the pool to see bottom except in strong sunlight.

Up above, things went badly. The river was running higher than I thought and it was hard to get the fly down, and hard to wade in many places. One fish took me on the far side of the top pool, but he was chasing the fly as it came out of the slacker water and it pulled out of his mouth. I saw him as he turned back and thought he was dark. Another fish took beautifully in the pool on the flat, but he was already spawned and very sluggish; the weight of the current carried him a long way below me and I found myself blocked from following by the branches of a big alder that hung twenty feet out over the stream, so had to work him slowly and painfully back before I could release him. In the next two pools I found nothing at all, which was natural enough as the river was too high for them to fish properly from the side I was on. So I came to the Cedar Stump Pool, fishless and not too impressed with my choice of a day.

The pool fishes fast because it is so straight and so narrow. One wades in at the head, to get clear of the steep bank and the tangle of brush along it, makes a few short casts partially upstream to fish the head, and in almost no time the fly is hanging opposite the cedar stump, sixty feet below. That's probably just as well, because the head is never productive, and the suddenness with which the fly comes to the holding water makes one pause and work the cast again, just to make something out of the pool. I had a double reason for doing so on this day, because I thought I felt a faint pluck as the fly crossed by the stump.

I got the fly deeper on the second cast and felt the pluck again; almost a pull this time, but still something less than a definite take. I wondered about the possibility of a cedar limb wedged in the bottom, so that the fly just touched it on the swing. Twice more I cast and each time felt the faint interference. Then I let the fly swing over too far at the end of the cast and hooked a submerged alder limb. I could not free it from where I was standing, so went down.

When I had the fly again I stood for a moment wondering whether to go back up and try the lie once or twice more. I believed what I had felt had been a fish, but supposed my fly hadn't been working deep enough or slowly enough, so decided to make an upstream cast. I made an awkward roll to get out line straight in front of me, so that the fly landed on the far edge of the current, right in line with the stump, and whipped straight across. I could see it, almost dragging the surface, and I saw the fish roll easily up and take it.

It seemed the answer to a fisherman's prayer in such a place, because the strike came at once from the swinging line from downstream, and the fish went hard against it up to the head of the pool. I judged her to be a small female, not over eight pounds, and I had seen she was reasonably bright. She was holding now in midcurrent, twenty yards above me, obviously swimming quite hard, so I kept a good strain on. It seemed reasonable to suppose she would tire enough to be content to stay in the pool and give me a chance.

I don't remember how long she held there or what started her down; probably I grew impatient and put on too much strain. She came suddenly, and very fast, right down the center of the pool. For a moment the line was slack, then she came hard against the reel and in another moment the backing splice went out. She was well beyond the tail of the pool now, but I still thought she might stop, and fifty yards of backing were gone before I began to stumble after her through the deep fast water. She was still taking line around the curve of the rapid when I came to a hanging alder and decided to ride past it on tiptoe. There was another alder below with limbs that pushed still farther out over the stream, but she was still running and the thin little spool of backing left on the reel gave line so unwillingly I had to help it with my hand; so I took a chance on the second alder and half-floated past that. I knew I had to get out then or swim a rugged trip through the rapid, so I struggled back towards the bank. As I got there I realized she had stopped running.

I rested for a moment on the edge of the stream because I was sweating and mildly winded. The thin backing stretched down into the broken water at a depressingly long angle and I warned myself that there was no reason to suppose it might still be holding a fish. I also decided I had grossly deceived myself about the size of this particular fish; she must be, I thought, all of fifteen pounds, and that was conservative. If the truth were known she was probably better than twenty.

There were alders fifteen or twenty feet high all along the edges of the rapid and for a moment I thought I must either break and lose my fly line, or else take the trip down the rapid after all. Then I realized that the bank sloped sharply up to a bench at least as high as the top of the alders. I climbed out and went up. By walking logs and climbing on to strategic stumps I managed to clear the line over the tops of the alders. The fly seemed to be wedged in something solid on the far side, just under the head of the long shallow reach. Things were easier now and I got downstream of whatever was holding the fly and went back to the river. Then I pulled quite hard. There was a great disturbance in the shallow water and I knew I still had my fish. I also supposed I must have been muddle-headed when the fish took, because the fish I had now was obviously red, and huge.

After the first plunge my fish went back to holding, so I waded out into the fast, even, two-foot depth of the shallow and put on more pressure. The fish came back, obviously tiring, but I knew my only hope of beaching her was on the far side, so I waded on across. Then I saw her, still very bright, an eight-pound female.

And following her, in close solicitude, was an enormous, red-sided, hook-jawed male. She got below me again, of course, and made a clumsy affair out of what should have been a tidy beaching. And the male followed her, close around my legs, right into water so shallow he scared himself and started out again. But I could see him waiting no more than twenty feet away while I worked to free the hook. She was bright, and in good condition, and we needed fish at home. But with anthropomorphic sympathy I carried her back to the water and held her while she recovered. The male waited while I did so, swinging to within two or three feet of her without a sign of fear. And he followed when at last she swam away.

Fly Types

THERE ARE SAID TO BE MORE THAN thirty thousand "recognized fly patterns" in circulation. I am not sure what constitutes a recognized pattern, but presumably it is one whose name and dressing have appeared in print. I am quite sure I could not name more than half the flies in my own fly boxes, and that is true also of most fishermen I know. And I have tied and forgotten many more patterns and variations than I have ever bothered to name, even though most of them caught fish before I forgot them. So it is reasonable to suppose that the figure of thirty thousand does not begin to represent the enormous multiplicity of creation that goes on among fly tiers.

One thing I do feel fairly sure of is that there aren't a thousand, much less thirty thousand, creatures of major interest to trout.and salmon for all these creations to imitate or represent. Fortunately, the fish don't seem to realize this and they go on chasing and grabbing any combination of hair and feathers we decide to mix together on a hook; so we can go cheerfully on flattering ourselves that we've worked out one more way of fooling them, and secretly hoping that somewhere out of the mess we may happen on that surefire artificial that really knocks 'em dead under any and all conditions.

The surest sign that we haven't done so, and never will, is in this very multiplicity of named and available patterns. If all the searching had turned up one or two or half a dozen patterns markedly superior to all the rest, fishermen would cleave mainly unto these and let the others lose themselves in the recesses of reference libraries. Instead, they go on searching, whether they tie flies or merely buy them, and let the confusion grow until no man can know what he should take with him to the waterside or leave behind in the tackle box.

Personally I think it is all good clean fun, and a thoroughly deserved tribute to the excellence of a trout's eyes and the receptive quality of the huge optic lobes in the brain behind them. Make no mistake, trout do see well. They are designed to see well and their lives depend on seeing well; they must see well both to escape danger and to select food. They can also distinguish between colors, whether or not they see colors as colors. These things are demonstrable and have been demonstrated, but it is altogether possible that the excellence of a trout's eyes, functioning in the medium to which they are adapted, has qualities of perception beyond these easily imagined ones. Certainly they can see to find feed in what to humans would seem total darkness.

Yet they are constantly being persuaded into taking artificial flies that vary all the way from delicately faithful reproductions of their natural food to outrageous misrepresentations of everything that nature stands for. It may well be that they fail to reject the latter because they are unaware of any need to. There must be many firsts in a trout's life, most of them with pleasant associations; the first mayfly, the first sedge and stonefly and chironomid, the first bee or yellow jacket or flying ant, the first moth, the first big, hairy caterpillar, the first sculpin or stickleback or baby trout. In all waters that have not been too heavily fished, the weight of conditioning must suggest, as some bright monstrosity comes floating by, "Try it." So the trout does, and one more successful artificial is born.

I am not a mathematician, but when I remember this and think of the enormous variety of materials available to the fly tier, it is obvious that the end product can only be infinity. And the answer to the fisherman's prayerful question, "What fly shall I use?" lies not in knowing his way among the thirty thousand named varieties, nor in searching through infinity, but in developing for himself some logically based system of selection that allows him to bring order out of one corner of chaos and go about his business with some measure of confidence.

For the man who believes in natural imitation and fishes a single type of stream with known and regular hatches, the problem is a fairly simple one. The dry-fly purist of the English chalk streams, for instance, probably will follow Halford or Dunne or one of the other masters, or perhaps work out his own combination from among them. I have known good chalk stream fishermen who insisted they could do all that was necessary with only two contrasting flies in various sizes—a Tup's Indispensable and a Halfstone, one said; light variant and dark, said another. I should want more leeway than this, but I'm not at all sure it would catch me more fish.

To a lesser extent, the same is probably true of most waters where brown trout are in the majority and fishermen are numerous. Easterners can follow Gordon or Jennings or Hewitt and be sure of safe guidance. They can, of course, elect to become lost among the fantasies of California, the aberrations of Oregon and the improbabilities of Washington and British Columbia; but unless they fish a diversity of streams they need not and probably had better not.

Here, in the wide and unsophisticated waters of the West, the problem is a little different. Fish and fishing are in such variety, experience has been so little accumulated and explained that one has to feel one's way around. And that is a dangerous admission, because it is all too likely to lead back into the middle of chaos, or beyond that into infinity. It won't do. There must be something the mind can grasp and the fly box contain.

My own solution, when I am being serious and not experimental, is to think of fly *types* rather than patterns. Then, having made my choice of the type or types of fly I want to fish, I try to have a fair choice of color or shape within the type.

What I mean is most easily shown in the case of winter steelhead fishing. It is safe here to rule out floating flies or the slim low-water flies that fish up in the surface film, unless one is out to experiment. That leaves the true wet fly. But there are still several types of this; there is the traditional strip-wing, built-wing or whole-feather-wing fly generally used for Atlantic salmon; the hackle fly; the hair flies, including optics and humpbacks and other distortions that weight the fly or give it unusual movement; and still others.

I have little difficulty in selecting among these, because everything I have seen of winter steelhead suggests to me that where the fly is put and how it is worked are infinitely more important than its color or shape or size. So I can afford to settle for a single type. I want to work my fly with a minimum of artificial movement across or against the current. So I prefer a feather type to a hair type. If winter steelhead have a color preference, I am satisfied it is orange, which confirms me in choice of feathers rather than hair; whole-feather tippets of golden pheasant give the best orange I know, though I usually compromise here by enclosing a little dyed orange bear fur between them, and the body can be orange again or gold tinsel, or bright green for all I care. Because a man needs an occasional change

86

for his own morale, I set against this a dark fly, like Thunder and Lightning or Blue Charm. And that is the end of the story. Not that I mind carrying and using other flies; I always carry them and often use them, and I tie experimental patterns, but they are no serious problem to me. As Kipling did not say, the more I know of the others, the more I settle to one.

With general trout flies the problem is not nearly so simple as this, but thinking in types still helps. There are the two main types, dries and wets, floaters and sunk flies. Among wet flies I think of the "traditionals," tied with strip wings or soft hackles; the minnow or streamer type, the hair type, the slim-bodied, low-water type, and nymphs. One could extend this by separating the heavy-bodied sedge type, the flexible-winged dredge type, the demon or terror type, but that gets complicated again and seems unnecessary. The first two fit in readily enough with the traditionals, and the third belongs with the minnows.

Among dry flies the groupings are similar. I think of the traditionals as the split-wing or hackle flies, tied with stiff, bright feathers. Closest to these are the spent wings, fan wings and parachute wings; then the sedges, tied with wings laid along the body and hackles ahead of the wings, the hair flies, and the terrestrial flies that imitate bees, ants, caterpillars and other land insects and so are likely to have cut hackles.

This alignment of types is arbitrary and fairly personal. Most fly-fishermen will have their own groupings, their own selections within them and their own feelings about the relative importance of the various

87

types. My only thought is to suggest a system for finding a way among the multiplicity of fly patterns and to give some idea of how it works.

If, for instance, I were going to fish a landlocked coast stream or lake for rainbows and cutthroats in summer, I should think mainly of dry flies. And my main choice would be hair patterns of a fairly large size—probably 8 and 10 hooks—with a fair color range; perhaps blue, gray, brown, green, orange and yellow. Supporting these, for a difficult fish, I would have a few well-tied traditionals such as Ken Cooper ties in Detroit, probably variants on 12 or 14 hooks. And I should certainly carry a few dry sedges, some derivative of the western bee, and perhaps one or two other terrestrial imitations. I might or might not slip in a couple of minnow flies to give me a chance at a big fish chasing a small fish I had hooked.

If I were fishing a migratory stream in the fall, I should still think mainly of dry flies and mainly of the big deer-hair patterns. I should not be much concerned with the small variants, though I might take them. And I would certainly carry two or three gray Wulff Atlantic salmon flies, because I use these to search badly broken water; fish do not always take them faithfully, but they often roll at them and reveal themselves for another offering. I should take also a selection of slim-bodied wet flies, chiefly of the minnow type, with the thought of steelhead, coho salmon and coho grilse. I have occasionally risen the first of these to a dry fly, but never the other two; and there are always some big cutthroats that simply will not have a floating fly.

These two examples are enough to show how the system works. The idea is to type flies by their effect and performance, to select the types that will match the problems the fish are likely to present, and to have a reasonable, but not excessive, range of choice within each type. There are waters, I know, where a really wide range within a single type may be important. There are times when one pattern takes every fish that rises and the others move nothing. But even on these special and by no means frequent occasions, I am quite sure that half a dozen equally successful patterns could be found if one had the time to search for them. And I am equally sure they would not all be recognizably similar to the human eye.

Trout are well-equipped to distinguish between flies, and they do react differently to different flies; they may disregard one completely, splash at another, come short to a third, take a fourth with calm and utter confidence. Sometimes, though not often on Pacific Coast streams, they can feed with rigid selectivity. They can and do become educated to the point at which they will respond only to the most faithful representation of a natural—or to some startling departure from it. But when all this is admitted, I think it is easy to give them too much credit for wisdom and cunning. They have to eat to live. They are guided by reflexes, not by conscious and logical thought. On a familiar hatch that suits them well, the reflex may become grooved and the fisherman had better take this into consideration; he may have to match size or color or form, or possibly all three. But as a general rule he need only conform to the probabilities, and not always to these, to stir the reflex action.

The important things in fishing are such matters as keeping out of sight, presenting the fly so that the fish can see it; giving it a chance to float naturally without drag, if dry; or swimming it with a stimulating action if wet, always on gut light enough to be unnoticed and to leave the action free. Only after these things is the pattern of the fly important.

Because a fish eats to live, and because most streams produce a good variety of offerings, absolutely selective feeding is rare. And provided the probabilities are reasonably covered, a fish is likely to choose a large fly in preference to a small one. It is reasonable to match the large fly either to the color of the small fly of the main hatch or to that of the few larger flies that will be coming down. But it is probably not essential to do so in most cases, because there are almost certain to be other types of feed acceptable to the fish.

I realize that this cuts rather sharply across popular dry-fly theory, and I would never suggest that such ideas should be overworked on extremely difficult waters like Silver Creek in Idaho, or the heavily fished eastern streams or some of the English chalk streams, though even in these waters they have some application and the wise fisherman applies them. In western waters fishermen apply them constantly, both knowingly and unknowingly. I know many men who have a great fondness for spent-wing flies and who fish them consistently and successfully without the slightest concern as to whether or not there are any spent spinners on the water. I can't see a reason in the world why they should not do so, because our trout are perfectly willing, as often as not, to take a spent-wing artificial from amongst an unvarying procession of natural duns. Whether they do so because they cannot tell the difference, or because they can tell the difference, is anybody's guess.

Similarly, most western dry-fly men regularly fish flies several sizes larger than the preponderant hatch, and catch more fish than they would with smaller flies. This also makes sense, since the trout rarely disregard a large natural mayfly that comes down amongst a heavy hatch of smaller ones. And the visibility and floating qualities of the larger flies are extremely important to the angler's comfort and efficiency on rough streams.

In rough and broken water the big flies remain effective even after heavy fishing has educated the trout. In smoother waters this is less true; one has to turn to carefully tied flies with high quality hackles. It is not always necessary to match the size, or even the color of the natural, but it is necessary to present a fly that behaves naturally, that sits up well on the water with the hackle points denting the surface film, not distorting it or piercing it. By the same token, a really well-tied fly, of high quality materials, will usually persuade unsophisticated trout, though it probably will not do better than a large fly of less perfect workmanship and materials.

I have several times mentioned imitations of terrestrial, as opposed to aquatic, creatures. These are important in the same way that the large mayfly imitations are important because trout, even large and educated trout, are very partial to the big and juicy offerings that drop to the water from bushes or blunder into it in clumsiness or flight. Such creatures are not designed to float daintily on the surface of the water, and they do not. They stir and struggle and sink down until they are only half-floating or completely submerged. Flies that imitate them are best tied clumsily, with unbalanced wings, cut hackles and other distortions of the fly tier's art. But the fisherman who uses them should be aware of what he is doing. If the trout reject or rise short to his cut-hackled bee yet take natural mayflies with calm regularity, he should be quick to change.

I have tried to suggest the sort of thinking by which I decide what flies I want with me. I am concerned to be ready for certain types of probability, and I think I can cover them best by carrying a few patterns of varying types rather than by many patterns of a single type. It should be possible to select no more than six patterns, work out dressings for them varying entirely by the types I have suggested, and go confidently about the business of catching trout. No fisherman is likely to do this, or if he does do it to stay with it, because even those of us with least excuse for doing so like to keep on searching for new and wonderful flies that trout will respond to with utter and unvarying confidence. That is part of being a fisherman. And even this foredoomed pursuit of the non-existent makes a little more sense if one pays attention to what effect the flies are intended to produce, and to the probabilities of a trout's behavior.

The Forecast

FISHERMEN HAVE ALWAYS TRIED TO calculate in advance their chances of sport, to use wind or weather, tide or time of day, temperature, barometer pressure or some combination of these and other factors to forecast that mystic hour when the fish will again be taking as they were on the remembered, golden day. Some few things have proved more or less predictable—the times of the hatches that produce sport on the mayfly streams, changes of tide and light that stir fish in salt water, the effect of a river's rise or fall, or of wind on a lake. We all use such things and to some extent try to guide our fishing by them. But fortunately for the charm of the sport even these affairs of directly visible cause and effect are not infallible; too many other factors can enter and make the improbable time better than the probable.

There is no shadow of doubt that conditions and fish do repeat themselves, and they do so together. The best possible means of forecasting sport is long experience and close observation, backed by an accurate written record. Unfortunately there is no short cut to this except skill in dealing with variables, an art that grows out of such difficult qualities as wisdom in choosing what to observe, utter faithfulness in observation, complete honesty and sharp intelligence in interpretation. Most happy fishermen are far too pleasant and easygoing to be able to lay claim to any such catalogue of virtues, so we learn slowly by an experience that falters often, goes chasing rainbows and nursing superstitions. But we do learn, unless we grow tired somewhere along the line and settle for the secondhand theories of experts who sell us the mathematics of tide and moon, of sun, wind, stars and barometer, sometimes with added mixtures of latitude, longitude, temperature and humidity for universal good measure.

Every so often friends present me with printed booklets of these calculations, and urgent requests that I study and use them. I have started out manfully on several occasions to do something of the sort, only to be brought up short by the enormously improbable picture of all the fish and game in the world moving twice daily in solemn unison to this rendezvous with death at the hands of the literate sportsman. There is, of course, a local variation, but it conforms to the time zones, and this seems to add a little to the unity of intent. Examining the thing still further, I find that the experts do not agree as to the precise hour or two of suicidal effort. And then, applying a rather harsh form of logic, I wonder why the proponents of all this precision do not seek to seduce me with neatly drawn graphs to show how exactly the total catch records of a few major waters, to say nothing of commercial landings, conform to the predictability of the fish. It would seem a simple matter to do so; I have known skeptics who were not above doing just this to prove the opposite.

The next thing that stops me is the reliance that most of the prediction experts place on the barometer. I kept a record of barometer readings on fishing days for some fifteen years, but have given up doing so because I could not find the slightest correlation between the vagaries of the barometer and the results of my fishing effort. I seem to catch fish equally well, or equally badly, on a rising, a falling or a steady barometer. I mentioned this to my friend, Tom Brayshaw, who is a mathematician as well as a fine fisherman.

"Why in hell should a fish worry about the barometer?" Tom asked. "If it drops an inch while you're out, all he's got to do is go down a foot in the water to find the same pressure. And if it rises an inch he can come up a foot."

At least, I think that's what he said. That or something very like it. And since I've watched fish swim quietly up through twenty feet of water to take a fly, I don't know why I bothered to record atmospheric pressure through all those years, nor why I should doubt the lack of effect my record shows.

Temperature is fairly important, but one can only make a few generalizations about it. I have caught steelhead on the fly in a fast stream where the temperature reading was a degree or more below freezing, and I have teased trout up to the fly in lakes with a surface temperature of over 70° F. It is a fair generalization that trout and salmon will prefer a temperature range between 45 and 60° F. if they can find it without upsetting too many other concerns. Fly-fishing in a lake will not normally be very good with a surface temperature much over 60° F., but in a fast-running stream the fishing can be excellent with the water at 70°. Fly hatches, presumably, are somewhat affected by temperature, but I think the effect is in long-term development of maturity rather than immediate. Every fisherman has seen midwinter hatches of mayflies. I have watched magnificent hatches in streams running at 35 to 40° F., when not a single trout would move up to them from the more comfortable waters of the lake below.

It is good to know these things, to test them occasionally, to understand the causes that are slowly working to stir or mature the eggs and larvae of insects, the eggs and alevins of fish. But it is bad to be ridden by them or so deeply convinced by some abstruse, not readily demonstrable theory that one stays home when there's a chance to go out. And what fisherman wants to be everlastingly dabbling a thermometer and wondering about results when he could be looking for fish?

I think the direct signs, the obvious effects, are immeasurably the most important. The times of fly hatches are often predictable, not from temperature studies or as a result of deep entomological study, but simply from careful observation. Annual movements of forage fish are often important and again are to some extent predictable. The height of both lakes and streams affects the movements and lying places of fish; six inches or a foot in the height of a stream can change a good feeding spot into a poor one, or vice versa; a couple of feet in the level of a lake can bring a whole new feeding area into use. Fish respond to these things as one would expect them to, and they don't wait for the moon or the tides, nor even the sun, wind and stars to be right.

Tides can be important. They are very important in estuaries and salt water, where their effect is direct. But just what is important about them will vary from place to place. I know estuaries where the trout usually take best on the last hour or two of the ebb, others where half-flood is usually best, others again where I have had good fishing at peak of high water. Out in the salt water, change of tide often stirs fish by setting currents into previously sheltered places, but the effect is not always from changes. Tide is always worth attention, and local knowledge is the best guide to its meanings.

Anglers have probably wasted more hours on early

morning fishing than on all other superstitions about their sport. Early morning can be a good time to go fishing, especially in salt water and in certain fresh-water bodies where there are powerful dawn and dusk movements of light-hating planktons and other creatures. But no power on earth would drag me out of bed even an hour earlier than usual to fish most trout waters, except for the sake of being out at a lovely time of day. Trout, it has always seemed to me, are aesthetically insensitive to this loveliness.

Evening rises are more profitable and dependable; besides, they entail no special effort or violation of comfortable habit. But they are far from infallible. If I wanted fish I would choose to fish most waters through the middle of the day rather than at early morning or late evening.

Many fishermen believe that brilliant sunlight is an adverse condition. It probably is, but it is far from being an impossible condition, even on a glass-still lake. I can remember hundreds of fish that have risen to my flies in brightest sunlight, and by no means all of them were unsophisticated. There was a cruising brown trout in the shallow eddy of a small clear stream; I had tried for him many times under more favorable conditions, but he came confidently to my fly at last in a hot, still August noon.

Thunderstorms are supposed to have an effect on fish. I believe they have, but it is several effects rather than a single one. I have had very good and very bad fishing, and sometimes indifferent fishing before, during and after thunderstorms. On the whole I am inclined to think thunderstorms are a good risk, more likely than not to produce interesting fishing at some stage of their wax and wane.

It is not hard to remember many days when one went fishing because it was convenient to do so, even though all the conditions seemed wrong, and found excellent fishing. I had a couple of hours to wait for a friend on a big lake last year. There was a strong hard wind, cold and unpromising, but I decided to fish anyway. At the mouth of the creek I had chosen there was a heavy swell and no sign of fish. I drifted on into the bay beyond, casting a wet fly occasionally towards shore, having difficulty with the boat because the water was still too open to the wind, and finding no fish. The shoreline ran in a series of bays, each deeper than the last, within a single big bay. There was more and more shelter until at last I found a bay with long smooth swells and only occasional gusts of wind to ripple them. A fish rose within reach, so I changed to a dry fly, covered him and rose him. He was a good fish and as I played him and netted him I noticed two or three other rises well-scattered about the bay. For the next hour I worked my dry fly, sometimes covering rises, sometimes dropping it in likely places. At the end of the hour I had eight fish over fourteen inches, and had returned half a dozen more.

On this same lake I have several times had the chance to move from creek to creek by airplane, a swiftness of travel little short in effect of being in several places at once. All the creeks are good and at some time in nearly every day there will be good rise at each of them. Yet, surprisingly often one finds fish feeding very actively at one, or perhaps two creeks, while the other four or five are absolutely quiet. So far as I am concerned this is satisfying proof that purely local conditions are far more important than any system of calculations designed to show a daily movement, mysteriously co-ordinated by remote universal factors.

But I have a far more serious objection than any of these to rigid systems forecasting the behavior of fish. It seems to me the fisherman carries an abundance of mental hazards within himself and has no need to add to them. If he is not catching fish he can, and undoubtedly will, wonder if his fly is wrong, his gut too heavy or his choice of pools unsound; he will wonder if the hatch is too late or the day too bright or the river too high or his casting too clumsy. If he must also remember that the mystic tables say the time is too late or too early, he can hardly be expected to fish on with even a remnant of confidence. Worse still, if he is a very faithful believer, he may consult the oracle before he goes out and may decide to stay home, though the day is lovely and spring is in the woods and fish are rising all over the river.

The time to go fishing is when the chance comes. And the way to go is with a free and hopeful mind, and an eye quick to take note of things. There will be days when the fishing is better than one's most optimistic forecast, others when it is far worse. Either is gain over just staying home.

The New Rod

My FRIEND, LETCHER LAMBUTH, made me a rod. Not because I had asked for one or because he knew I had desperate need of one, but rather because he believed I was a fit person to own a Lambuth rod. He announced it with a casualness out of all proportion to the event. "Your rod is almost finished. You must pick it up when you come down in the fall."

A Lambuth rod is an event, chiefly because of Letcher's meticulous care and craftsmanship and because of the effort he has devoted to understanding just what makes a fine rod. For many years we have taken him our rods to be calibrated, tested for vibration, deflection, balance and many other factors. Letcher has translated all this information into curves and plans, then matched each rod's mathematics against the owner's subjective account of its performance. From the mass of interrelationships has grown his understanding of what and why a fly rod is.

The rod he made for me is nine feet long and weighs five and three-eighths ounces. It is of cane that he himself bought and seasoned and split. The guides and fittings are simple and light. In gluing, the cane sections have been spiraled one-sixth of a turn for every foot of the rod's length, which gives a theoretical and actual increase of twelve per cent in power and strength for weight. The rod remains supple and responsive in spite of this, adaptable to any reasonable use, with the quality that good rods have of becoming an extension of the hand and arm that uses them, muscular, sympathetic and sensitive.

If Letcher's rods were far less good than they are, I should still value this one above all my other rods because of Letcher's quality as a fisherman. He is a man of gentle precision, extremely skillful with his hands and with a mind that sorts detail into place and forces meaning from it; he has a scientist's touch, a scientist's objective honesty, a scientist's devotion to inquiry and experiment. Yet he is also a man of intense and glowing enthusiasms, and in a quiet, disarming way he carries almost everyone else along on his enthusiasms. He hardly ever uses the pronoun "I"; it is always "we," and the we is made to include the person spoken to, even though he may have done nothing towards the enthusiasm under discussion at the moment. When Letcher talks to me of building rods, he says "we" and somehow includes me, though I have never split a piece of bamboo in my life and would not think of starting out to make a split-cane rod. When he speaks of his fine collection of western trout-stream insects and the flies that imitate them, his "we" somehow includes every honest fly-fisherman on the Pacific Coast; when he speaks of conservation, "we" means every fisherman who ever trod a stream bank or sat in a boat or dangled his feet from a rock.

Letcher is a quiet and skillful fisherman, far less concerned with the death or capture of fish than all his devotion to the theory of these things would suggest. For some years his eyesight has been very bad, so bad that he cannot read nor see things at all clearly at a distance. He cannot make rods or identify insects, yet he continues both interests with as strong an enthusiasm as ever. He is carefully committing his knowledge of rod-building to the care of his friends who have the skill to use it. And his collection of insects and imitations continues to grow, matched and identified by other eyes than his, those of his wife Olive or one of his friends, but raveled into meaning by himself. When he goes fishing he wears breast waders and uses them; "we" tell him how the river bottom is ahead of him, what is the strength of the current, where he must turn back to avoid a bad place. We may tell him, too, that the far bank has many overhanging bushes and the fish are lying close under them. He will fish the pool as faithfully as any of us, setting his fly within inches of the bushes at every cast, hanging it in them far less often during the length of the day than our arrogance of eyesight leads us to. It is Letcher, too, who makes the meticulously measured and calculated old-fashioneds when we get home in the evening or even, sometimes, mixes them beside the river at noon.

My Lambuth rod means all this to me, and much more. And it did so from the start, so I resolved to enter it with care and use it with unfailing caution and respect. It is a trout rod, supremely comfortable to fish with either wet fly or dry, as a good rod should be. It is a rod with which to look for two- or three-pound trout and hope for five-pounders, yet it is sensitive enough to give even a twelve-inch fish a chance to perform, or to handle a big fish on 4x gut. But it is not a rod to expose to salmon-size fish such as steelheads, especially in fast water.

I chose a small Vancouver Island stream in April for its introduction to fish, and the first fish was almost worthy of the rod. I found her behind a big rock at the head of a bright and lovely pool, a three-and-a-quarter-pound cutthroat, handsomely colored but fully recovered from the spawning of the previous winter. She was by far the largest cutthroat I have had in good condition so far from salt water at that time of year, and I felt grateful to her for her good recovery; a thin and flabby fish would have been a disappointment on such an occasion.

Later in the day we were at the Shepherd's Pool, expecting the lively pound or pound-and-a-half cutthroats that run up there for the dog salmon fry. Lee Richardson was with me, hoping for photographs—Lee claims to go fishing and often puts on waders, but a rod would be terribly in his way and a couple of fly boxes piled on top of his camera equipment would probably burden him beyond further movement. Yates Hickey, who was with us, had gone down to the next pool with his four-ounce Leonard and the determination that sometimes comes on Yates to go catch a fish when everyone else is wasting time.

I can't remember about the cutthroats, whether they were there or not. But I remember a solemn, solid rise to my fly in the deep run under the far bank and the grim realization that I was fast in a big steelhead. In the same moment there was a wild yell and a wave from Yates.

"What does he say?" I asked Lee.

"He's got a steelhead," Lee said, unlimbering his camera. "I better go down there."

"So've I," I said. "May as well stay here. It's a lousy kelt though, and his will be, too."

My fish was big, red and long and lazy as I had feared he would be, the sort of log of a fish that a precious rod should not be called upon to fool with. But he was unexpectedly co-operative. He ran to the tail of the pool, then turned and swam lazily upstream. I went into the eddy and let him go, then he let me lead him back down between me and the bank. I slipped my boot under him, slid him luckily onto the gravel and in a moment the hook was out. Lee watched and took photographs as I urged the fish into swimming away.

"Yates is still yelling," he said, and we hurried down.

Yates was excited as he seldom is. "He's taken me twice down the pool and jumped all over it and now he's gone again. Nearly two hundred yards of line out. I'll never get him back up."

The pool was very long and narrow, and fast all the way, under a high cut-bank. "Boy," Yates said. "Is this ever a dandy! Bright as a dollar. Most fun I ever had."

Lee was taking pictures. The fish was coming back, still strongly, against the current. And Yates humored him perfectly, almost dancing with pleasure and using every ounce of the tiny rod. Then the fish was wobbling, half on its side, in the narrow strip of quieter water just over from the pool's head. I went in, got below it, gripped tail and gill covers and lifted it out.

She was obviously a female, about ten pounds, deep

and thick, silver-sided, green-backed, one of the prettiest steelheads I have ever seen.

"Don't tell me she's a kelt," Yates said.

I looked at the fins. Not one was frayed or worn. The vent was not swollen. There was no visible roughness at the edge of the scales, no scars or marks of any kind except a round bruise, smaller than a fifty-cent piece, at the wrist of the tail. We killed her and it was perfectly all right to do so. She had spawned, but her flesh was firm and pink and thick as that of a fresh-run fish.

Two or three weeks later, in early May, I took the Lambuth rod to the Islands Pool with Tom Brayshaw. "There won't be any kelts up there," I said. "Not this late." I was looking for the spring run of little two- and three-pound steelheads.

The river was very high and there was thick gray silt coming down the near side from work they were doing on the dam. We waded out with difficulty and Tommy's thigh boots would not take him beyond the stained water. My waders did better and I worked up in the shelter of a big rock and began to fish. Within two or three casts I hooked a huge kelt and for twenty minutes the Lambuth rod had to do everything a respectable trout rod should not be asked to do. Finally Tommy netted the fish for me behind the convenient shelter of a stranded fir stump. I looked anxiously at the rod. It was as straight and even as it had ever been. So I waded out again and immediately hooked a bright six-pounder that raced all over the tearing water and jumped like a coho. I lost him in the end because the fly came away, but once again the rod had done more than its share—and still it was straight and perfect. So I tried again and caught the two-pounder I had been looking for in the first place.

It was two months after that before I gave the rod its proper fishing chance, in a quick little dry-fly stream among fourteen- and sixteen-inch fish. I still don't take it out to look for steelhead or salmon except in lowest summer water. But if a ten-pounder chooses to take hold in heavy water when I am about my business— well, that's his affair. I am no longer worrying about the rod.

Fly Lines

IT IS A FLY-FISHER'S AXIOM THAT HIS lines are the most important part of his equipment, and I suppose this has remained constantly true from the days of the loop rod and the twisted horsehair line, through the development of silk and vacuum dressing, to this present age of nylon and multiple tapers.

In fly-fishing the line does most of the work. It must be heavy enough to use the action of the rod and carry the fly out accurately to a fair distance; it should be smooth enough not to tangle when looped in the hand; it must be light enough to fall gently near the fly; it must float or sink in accordance with the fisherman's desires and intentions; and it must be adaptable to the

various casts he may wish to make—overhand or underhand, roll or angle, spey or double spey, short or long
or in-between.

The double-tapered, vacuum-dressed, oiled-silk line
was the natural development of all these needs. It is
just thirty years since I owned my first one, and no
other single thing in my fishing life has been comparably
important. It made the whole difference between dabbling a fly over bushes or under bridges and going out
fly-fishing. Thousands of boys before me had learned
to fish admirably with silk lines and hemp lines and
hair lines, variously treated or untreated, tapered or un-
tapered. But I believe I came into the thing when the
fly line had reached the peak of its development, and
my transformation into a fisherman was easier for that.

I have owned many fly lines since that first one, including level lines, torpedo heads and multiple tapers.
But I am satisfied that for all normal fly-fishing pur-
poses a good double taper, well cared for and accurately
balanced to the rod it is used with, is beyond improvement and far beyond need of improvement.

The point is worth discussing because of the enormously increased use of torpedo and multiple tapers
since the war. Both these lines are developments of
tournament casting. They have heavy bellies, of comparatively short length, set well forward and backed
by a good length of thin running line—for shooting,
not casting. The multiple-taper line is better balanced
and more scientifically designed than the simple torpedo
head—its graduated tapers are calculated to give a maximum carry of line in the air (usually forty to fifty feet)

followed up by a shoot of almost the same length when needed. Both lines are designed for use with light, stiff rods, of great power for their weight. And the multiple taper magnificently fulfills the very limited function for which it is designed; it allows an enormous length of line to be thrown with a light, stiff rod.

The only trouble with this, from my point of view, is that I rarely want to cast an enormous length of line with a light, stiff rod, and I want to do a great many other things that short, stiff rods and multiple-taper lines will not do with any degree of ease or comfort.

I have reached this conclusion rather cautiously because I do not want to be considered conservative and ancient. I thoroughly enjoy casting a multiple-taper line for a short while, but the fun goes out of it very quickly. It is fascinating at first to feel the strong pull of the line in the air, to watch the narrow loop shoot forward like a bullet and straighten out perfectly, dragging coil after coil of line from the hand behind it. Into a wind the performance is especially showy and feels especially good. But watching someone else at it, one quickly sees the flaws—the awkward, heavy-handed rod movements, the forcing of power into the cast. Style is gone, what should be easy and smooth and graceful has suddenly become jerky and awkward and full of strain.

In fishing, the disadvantages become even more obvious. Some lies may be reached that were beyond reach. But the fly is then way out there, somewhere off on the end of that thin running line, and there is little control because the thin line will not lift the heavy belly of the taper. When the fish takes, it is probably a matter of sheer luck if the hook goes home. When the cast is fished out, all that length of running line must be brought back into the hand before another cast can be made.

One moves on downstream. The river narrows, or there is a lie close in, calling for a short cast. One can make it, but awkwardly, because the limited length of line draws little response from the stiff rod. Now there are trees close behind and no room for a back cast. A double spey works only fairly well, rolling and shooting far less line than it should because the action of the rod is not sympathetic to it. A fish is hooked—again one has the stiff little rod, the tiring awkwardness, the power with lightness that gives only clumsy control.

This is looking on the dark side. One can make the outfit perform, make it stand up and do tricks, even make it feel and seem easy and graceful to use. But it remains specialized gear, somewhere midway between fly casting and bait casting, between fly-fishing and tournament casting. It does a wonderful job of throwing a fly a long way with a light rod, but does nothing else as well as the ordinary double taper will.

Since the war I have seen many fishermen come from the tackle stores armed with multiple-taper lines, yet having no conception at all of the theory of using them; they find them clumsy and difficult, and small wonder. I have seen others, skilled in their use, who were utterly at a loss when the river gave them no room for a back cast; and yet others who could get a fair performance from the gear, though nothing better than they could have had from softer rods and double-taper lines with a fraction of the effort.

This convinces me that the multiple taper is fine for the man who fishes a single type of river, in a rather specialized way, and thoroughly knows his business. For most fishermen, and for all-around fishing, where one is alternating many types of cast and aiming at close control of the fly, I think the double taper is still the better tool. An easy style is one of the most important pleasures in fishing, and this alone would be enough to swing the balance.

I used to believe in rather heavy fly lines, often a size heavier than the maker recommended for the rod I was using. I now think I was wrong in this. I seem to be able to get a far more satisfying performance from a line that is a fraction light for the rod than from one that is too heavy. I may not be able to cast so far, especially against a heavy wind, but I have better and more delicate control.

Care of lines remains a problem. A properly dressed silk line, unless it is constantly watched, will sooner or later go tacky. Nylon is the answer to this; one can put it away and forget about it. But nylon has a still more serious fault: the line will stretch while the dressing does not, so after a little use the dressing on a nylon line becomes broken and patchy. I used to think it was hard to keep a nylon line floating, but the new silicone dressings overcome this handsomely. The weight of a nylon line for its size seems to fall about midway between that of a silk line of the same size and the next smaller size. Because of this, one occasionally finds that a nylon line fits a given rod more closely than any silk line. When this happens I use the nylon line and enjoy it. But I don't expect it to last as long as a silk line would with reasonable care; in fact, I expect to have to turn the taper after one season of moderate use.

Probably some other synthetic material will overcome this matter of stretch, or perhaps a dressing will be found with equal stretch. I think the future is with synthetic lines rather than silk because of the deterioration of silk lines in storage. Even those of us who fish all through the year rarely do so with the same fly lines. A silk line can be safely stored in loose coils in a dark place, but, sooner or later, one leaves it coiled on the reel too long and it becomes tacky. That, so far as I am concerned, is the end of it. There are things that can be done to restore it, but they are troublesome things and the results are rarely satisfactory.

I have no solution for the problem that many of us pose for ourselves by switching from wet-fly fishing with a sunken line to dry-fly or greased-line fishing other than to carry two lines, one greased, one dry, on separate reels or drums. Even so, one is seldom willing to stop fishing and make the change. All such complications and problems of decision tend to detract from the pleasant simplicity of fly-fishing. Occasionally I have carried a multiple-taper line on a spare drum with the idea of using that when conditions were right for it, but it is a similar complication and similarly undesirable.

Fly lines are pleasant things, pleasant to the touch and the eyes as well as in use. A good one, balanced to the rod and in good condition, makes for good fishing as well as good casting. If an extra few yards of distance were the only factor, or even a major factor, I should probably use a multiple taper far more than I do. I believe that distance is rarely a major factor in finding or pleasing the fish, though often of importance in pleasing the fisherman. The ready adaptability of one's outfit to all types of cast and all conditions of fishing is to me the most important factor both in my personal pleasure and the effectiveness of my fishing. So I am still for the double taper, and I will even go to the length of carrying two of them most of the time, one greased, the other ungreased.

I have always been a fisherman, never a tournament caster, so it occurred to me that I might be missing some virtue of the multiple taper through simplicity or ignorance. With this in mind I asked a friend, the representative of a large tackle firm, an old tournament caster and a fine fisherman: "How do you feel about the multiple tapers? Do you use them? For fishing, I mean?"

He looked at me with a slow smile that clearly doubted the sincerity of my question. "What do *you* think?" he asked in return. "Do *you* use them?"

A Boy and a Fish Pole

I HAVE BEEN ASKED MANY TIMES BY anxious parents, usually fathers, "How do you start a boy out fishing?"

As it stands there, the question is a fair one and it shall have its answer. But far too often it is accompanied by some revealing addition, such as, "I never had a chance to learn it right and I'd like to see him do better," or, "A boy needs some good healthy sport like fishing to keep him out of trouble."

Anyone who hopes to push a boy into fishing "because it's good for him" or "to keep him out of trouble" is probably doomed to disappointment. So is the man

who hopes to realize in his son his own frustrated am-
bition to become a fine fisherman. Boys go fishing
because they want to go, and they become good fishermen because they enjoy fishing—not because being so
will be a help in business or a valuable hobby or a useful relaxation. And no one is quicker than a boy to
recognize the fact that something is being wished on
to him.

Going fishing with the old man, being made to pay
attention and pack the landing net and struggle to keep
up is, for most six-, eight- or even ten-year-old boys,
a form of purgatory sufficiently horrible to put them
off fishing for the rest of their lives. Small boys like
to roust around in their own way and in their own time.
They may or may not like to go along with the old
man and pay attention; let them choose, and don't let
anything but their own inclinations guide the choice.

My own thought with my own son so far—he is
now nine—has been to play the thing as honestly as
I know how. If I am going fishing he is more than
welcome to come so long as he looks after himself and
keeps happy. I often warn him that it may be cold
and dull and miserable, and I may not catch anything.
He usually comes, he usually has a wonderful time
fussing with his own affairs alone beside the river, and
pays only occasional attention to me. He sticks out discomfort with remarkable stoicism, and for the past three
or four years has been able to take himself off home
ahead of me from anywhere within walking distance.

But his happiest fishing times, and the times that
teach him most at this stage, are not with me, but when

he goes off on his own or with friends of his own age to poke around beaver dams or small creeks, dabble flies or spinners or worms, and catch occasional tiny fish. This is how a boy gets the feel of fishing and water and fish, how he finds the interest and grows into the enthusiasm.

It would not be true to say that I do not want him to be a fisherman. I believe fly-fishing to be the richest and most rewarding sport there is, and I should like him to find it as rich as I have found it and as rewarding. But I know many admirable and charming people who have never fished or tried to fish or wanted to fish, yet have had lives at least as full of pleasant and exciting things as my own; in addition, they are probably much more worthwhile people than I am for not having wasted so much time poking around rivers or arguing about flies or reading fish scales and fishing books. I try to remember this and keep a sense of proportion. If my Alan wants to be a fisherman, let me be there to help him; if not, let me be just as willing, if not as able, to help him to whatever it is he does want.

At the moment he seems to be interested in fishing, so my function will not much longer be passive. He begins to have some of the muscle and height he needs to handle a fly rod and get out into a stream. He has more and more the power of concentration that will let him hold to the business long enough to get some good out of it, a growing realization that fishing is long and pleasant spells of not catching fish. I have shown him the elementary timing of the overhead cast and he does well enough with it to tell me he knows how to cast and needs no more instruction. He will hold that thought for a while, as the muscles build and he finds out more for himself of what it is all about. Then he will want more and will come to me or some other friend to get it.

A father is not always the best teacher; in spite of his good intentions, he may be too exacting and too impatient, and he has to say so many things on so many subjects that what he says is not always given full value. Nor is the best fisherman always the best teacher—he has forgotten too much; too many of the things he had to learn have long ago become self-evident to him. But a father who uses himself carefully will be the best teacher a boy ever had, and a good fisherman who remembers that things were not always easy and rediscovers the ways they became easy can give as much as anyone.

Somewhere along the line discipline must enter. Not the psychologically softened, good mark for a good try insult to human character that often passes for discipline, but the put up or shut up, do it right or go home stuff that makes for performance. Most boys prefer it that way, understand it and accept the challenge. And lessons taught that way are learned so that they become part of a man and later save him the endless defeats of compromise and mediocrity. My own teachers taught me that way; and though I have since discarded or modified some of their teachings, I have done so without ever forgetting the principles that were behind the teaching.

So much for method. What to teach? The boy has learned for himself his interest in fishing, in lakes and streams or salt water; this is the product of the pottering and dabbling, the pole and string and bent pin, and it is the foundation on which the rest builds. He must learn enough of tackle to take proper care of it, to put it together and take it apart; he must learn enough of casting to give him a chance of being effective. After that—before it, during it and all through his life, for that matter—manners and sportsmanship are the important lesson. Neither can be learned in a day or taught by diagrams; both are matters of character rather than routine learning. But these are things to be taught, and proper learning of them has more to do with the sport's satisfactions than anything else.

All boys want to compete, and it is well that they should, but if they are to enjoy sport, as opposed to athletic contests, they must learn early to distinguish between the two. Sport is something enjoyed purely for its own sake, relaxing, healing and increasing; it is infinitely complex, limited in its scope only by the individual limitations of the man who pursues it; competition between men has no place in it and can only debase it. Athletic games and contests are competition between men; easygoing sportsmanship once had a part in such affairs, sometimes still has; but for the most part it is lost in ruthless efficiency and something called the will to win. Sport is carried on generously within the limits of simple and largely unwritten rules developed to make it more interesting; the hunter or fisherman who does not stay within these rules kills his sport. Athletic contests are carried to the extreme limits of rules rigidly designed to prevent manslaughter and reduce cheating; the modern athlete who does not take every possible advantage of the rules is considered a deficient performer. There is room for both diversions in a boy's life or a man's life or a nation's life, but there should be no confusion between them.

A boy may not be able to grasp these distinctions immediately, but they must be shown to him when he is young—as soon, in fact, as he starts serious fishing. He must learn without delay that the concern is always between him and the fish, never between him and another angler. He must learn that it is his business to be courteous and generous to extremes in all his encounters with his brother anglers by the waterside. He must learn that it is his business to understand as much as possible about the fish that make his sport, and to take responsibility for their perpetuation. He must learn that his pleasure is in fishing, not in killing; in the day and all its happenings rather than in a display of fish to vaunt his prowess; that his pleasure and his validity lie between himself and the God who made him, not in human approval or applause.

These things are not learned easily, and like other matters of spirit and mind they are best learned through example and influence rather than from direct teaching. But their rudimentary principles must be recognized and named. Good manners are worth emphasizing with the flat of the hand if necessary, and a boy who exceeds a bag limit and gets by with it is well on the way to becoming a menace.

These are the important things; without them the sport is nothing, a mere process of getting meat for the table or building one's ego at the price of a few dead fish. The boy who has understood the manners and ethics of angling, accepted them and made them a part of his thinking, is pretty well assured of the deepest satisfactions the sport can offer. He may break the unwritten rules—he probably will, because all boys are natural poachers—but it can do no harm if he knows he is wrong. Boys learn a lot from poaching, sometimes more than they learn from orthodox ways, and they often go to far more trouble to catch a fish by a questionable method than a legitimate one. If the solid principles of decent behavior have been absorbed, this is only gain; the faint qualms of conscience that assault the toughest mind effectively reduce satisfaction and confirm the earlier lesson.

It is wrong, I think, to teach fish and fishing as things isolated. Concentration is important; a fisherman must learn not to miss his opportunities. But it is important also to see the sport in its frame, which is the whole of nature. Nothing that moves or lives or exists within range of his vision and understanding is unimportant to a fisherman. Birds, trees, mammals, insects and weeds, weather and hills, meadows and rock and sky, are all part of a fisherman's world and his pleasure. In this again learning may be slow, through example rather than instruction. But the habit of observation and appreciation forms almost insensibly under the occasional questions, "Did you see this? Did you hear that? Did you notice something else?" The twelve-year-old may seem to have eyes and ears and other senses only for his fishing; the fourteen-year-old will have time to notice for himself; the sixteen-year-old may be quicker than his teacher—the man will have habit built in to him, a way of noticing his world that enriches his whole life.

These intangibles are the things that have to be taught, and it is the way they are taught and the way they are learned and used that makes the difference between a fisherman and a man with a fishing rod, or a boy with a fish pole. Any good caster can teach the elements of casting within a few hours; from then on practice is the best teacher. There are many things that any experienced fisherman can teach a boy about where and how to look for fish, how to judge water and hatches and feeding spells, about wading and keeping out of sight and setting the hook and using the landing net or gaff. All fishermen go on learning more of all these things from other fishermen all through their lives, and also go on proving and discovering more of them for themselves. A boy is entitled to this help, as much of it as can be given him. But in the last analysis his own keenness and enthusiasm must take over, to give the lessons life and meaning. And there is no sport better served by its literature than angling. A boy who is really interested can turn to hundreds of books that unfold the techniques and traditions and values of the sport with enormous competence and thoroughness, sometimes with deep insight. It is well that he should be shown this and taught the great names and great developments of the sport in proper proportion. He can then find his own place and part in the tradition of his sport, and he will have at hand a hundred teachers instead of one or two.

There is no substitute for going fishing, for the trial and error of learning that becomes experience. And experience, reflected and renewed, tested and proved and made a part of action, becomes one of the keenest joys of fishing. When a man can recognize the place and proportion of his own experience against the rich background of the sport, it has increased and intensified meaning. It is this *quality* of enjoyment and satisfaction, not mere proficiency, that a wise father wishes for his child. Good minds have always found it, because fishing is the richest and most complex of all sports, but it is not found in full measure without preparation. A man can learn for himself, even late in life, how to find it; but a boy, shown the right things early, will make them a part of himself and build on them through a lifetime of experience.

Northward Geese

THEO SAID THE FISHING WAS GOOD down in the tidal part of the river, so we went down in one of the boats from the lodge. It was a still evening and the tide was making a little at the piles; we stopped there a moment. I had a dry fly up and threw it into the draw of current around the first pile, without too much expectation. A good fish rose almost at once, but short. He would not come again.

I probably changed the fly soon after that. Certainly there was another rise, also well short, somewhere around the piles. But we went on down to the grassy island without a fish. We fished there idly, throwing in towards the island, seeing very few signs of fish. Theo told me of the new shotgun he had bought, an expensive gun of Belgian make with which he had been offered a case that cost almost as much as the gun. He had refused to buy the case; remembering some of my own bachelor extravagances, I was proud of him.

There was grebe in the slough, as there nearly always is, and we talked of that. A fish rose near the island and Theo covered him many times but nothing happened. About then I heard the geese calling. They seemed close and I thought they might be going to settle in at the mouth of the river for the night as they do even now, though people are all around and the log booms block most of the favorable water. It was quite a while before I could see them, very high and very far, a great flock of lesser snows streaming across the sky. They were beautiful in the stillness of the evening, as they always are, and seemed in a hurry. I always read some plan or wisdom into the flight of migrating geese and I thought: "They're trying to make some place before dark; Port McNeill, likely, or the mouth of the Cluxewe."

Theo was less interested in the geese than I was and more interested in the fish. He began to row the boat up the river, towards the piles. The sun had set but the sky was still light and there were long ripples of gold-edged clouds clear across it, very high. I heard geese again, the high, musical cry still loud and strong through the still evening; I knew how far to look this time and saw them at once, another great flock of wavys, strung in their shifting pattern across the clouds. While they were still in sight I heard another flock coming, and another.

"A fish rose in there," Theo said.

I looked quickly and saw the rings on the dark water, close under the bank below the first pile. "You try him," I said.

"No," Theo said. "It'll take too long. Throw at him yourself."

The boat was moving away, so I threw. It was a wet fly and I left it there for the movement of the boat to draw it. When it was almost straight behind the boat I retrieved a little line and he had it, deep down. He was a strong fish and all the while I played him the geese were passing. I thought I recognized lesser Canadas and cackling geese, as well as the wavys, from their voices, but they were all high, all hurrying, all in big flocks.

Theo netted the fish for me, a perfect estuary cutthroat of about a pound and a half. We were happy with him, satisfied with the evening, and Theo said, "I'll row on up towards the lodge, but keep fishing. I had a fish up here somewhere a night or two ago."

"Why don't you fish and let me row?" I asked him.

"Not worth changing over," he said. "It's almost dark." And it was, down there on the river, but not in the sky. And the geese were still passing. I could not always see them now but I could hear them, sometimes far out over the channel, sometimes almost overhead.

I kept casting, a little upstream and well out from the boat, letting the fly go down. A fish rose, a long way out, and I barely reached him with the fly. I felt him pluck at it, but missed him. So I cast upstream again and another one took me, deep down and solidly. He matched the first one almost exactly.

We had to pick up another boat on the way up to the lodge and Theo came with me to the house and we had a drink to a pleasant evening. So it was late, and quite dark, when I took the fish down to the river to clean them. There was no moon and only a few stars. Yet I heard geese hurrying through the black night above me as I walked down, heard others again while I cleaned the fish, and knew they were still passing while I walked back to the house. It's a good night, I thought, and they're using it. I wondered about that first flock. They would be past Cluxewe now, past the northern tip of Vancouver Island, heading out over Queen Charlotte Sound. On such a night, or in such a dawn as the next day's would be, they could pitch to rest almost anywhere. But I still wished I could know where it would be, in all that distance between the fiftieth parallel and the seventieth.

Stonefly Imitations

The stonefly nymph, "perla," is a great temptation to fly tiers. It lives in the good fast water that trout like, and in spring one finds it again and again in trout stomachs, standing out plainly among the clusters of smaller creatures and the broken debris of less well-constructed insects. *Perla* is a fine big nymph, usually with a mottled, dark brown back and a vividly contrasting pale olive-green belly; the body is flattened a little to work in the powerful currents of the rapids, and two long tails sweep back to tapered points.

Gordon tied a stonefly nymph for the Neversink, Jennings lists two dressings of his own, Ronald's has a dressing, Bergman shows a good one, and nearly all the authorities have them. Charles Cotton goes into the matter charmingly and at length, though with emphasis on the fly's winged phase. The wet march brown and the professor, in their larger sizes, must often have been taken by trout as stonefly imitations. In fact, the wet march brown, tied with yellow wool in the rear half of the body and the usual dark partridge wing, seems to me to have all the obvious essentials of the *Perla* nymph.

With all these one would seem to be well enough served. But *Perla* remains a temptation. It is so easy to imagine the big strong nymphs climbing over rocks in the fast water, being suddenly washed off and tumbled down to the waiting trout in alternating flashes of dark brown and greenish-yellow, or else swimming up towards the surface to break out their flat wings. That mottled brown of the back so urgently suggests golden pheasant tail feathers, and the other dressings don't give full recognition to the paleness of the underbody. A thick body would be better, olive seal's fur or primrose yellow or even bleached green, perhaps with ribs of gold to give it life. It must be worth trying. The nymph is so big and the trout so obviously like it; its abundance is at a time of year when one often wonders what fly to put up, and its behavior is the sort of thing that one can well reproduce with a properly controlled fly.

Of course, I've tried this dressing and many variations of it. They look fine, if I do say it myself, in the water and out. And they catch fish. But they don't work any miracles; I couldn't honestly say that they have done better for me than a march brown or a professor or any one of a dozen other flies would have. And when I stop to think about it, there isn't a reason in the world why they should.

Think of a pleasant day in April, a big cutthroat waiting at the head of the pool just below the rapids, anxious to feed. He has picked up half a dozen eggs, rolling down from steelheads spawning somewhere above him. Two or three salmon alevins, stirring too soon from the sheltering gravel, have been washed down in the same way to the same destination. A drowned beetle has appeared suddenly above him in the tumbled water and he has taken that, just below the surface. Then a mayfly nymph or two, another alevin, another beetle. And at last the stonefly nymph starts from the rocks, a few feet upstream of him. The current carries it as it rises through the water, the trout sees it and has it. Of course, why shouldn't he? But if another alevin had come, another drowned beetle, another steelhead egg, would he not have taken these as willingly? If a caddis grub, a drowned caterpillar, a drifting earthworm, an early ant or honey bee—any one of a dozen things not too removed from the general experience of his feeding—had chanced to come by, would he not have moved to them? From what I have seen of the contents of trout's stomachs, I'm reasonably sure he would have.

In most Pacific Coast streams the trout are rarely feeding selectively and when they are doing so the reason why is nearly always obvious. A flying ant hatch, a heavy run of salmon fry, occasionally a good hatch of mayflies can make close imitation a matter of urgent importance. In lakes, especially, there can be hatches of midge larvae that seem to hold the interest of every single fish while they last. But most of the time a feeding cutthroat or rainbow is likely to take anything from a drowned mouse to a free-swimming *callibeatis* nymph, from a four-inch bullhead to a four-millimeter snail. Trying for exact imitation of a *Perla* nymph simply because a few of them, whole, handsome and easily recognized, show up in trout stomachs, simply does not make sense.

By the same token, I do not believe that exact and careful tying of ordinary wet flies, either to pattern or form, is of any real importance in most of the fishing one does. If a trout's reactions are being tripped with equal facility by the appearance of a salmon alevin or a big black and yellow caterpillar, a mayfly nymph or a three-spined stickleback, he is not going to worry too much about the way I have set the wings on my *Perla* imitation—especially when the stage of *Perla* he is most likely to be interested in is still without wings. And I am foolish to suppose that, because I have reproduced a *Perla* nymph as exactly as feathers and fur and silk can do it, I shall work any miracles.

As a matter of fact, my *Perla* nymph of feathers can never be even nearly so faithful a reproduction—to the human eye—as a molded plastic model. Such a model could be made to reproduce shape and size and color so exactly that it would deceive the human eye completely. Yet it would not catch fish even nearly so well as my impressionistic combination of fur and feathers. Nearly every fly-fisherman's box holds some of these bright, stiff models of nymphs and shrimps and beetles and other such creatures, so lifelike to the human eye that they seem perfection. And in most fly-fishermen's boxes these creatures remain, year in, year out, unwetted and unswum. They are occasional conversation pieces and no more because they don't catch fish.

They don't catch fish because they don't trip the reaction. And they don't trip the reaction because they are stiff and lifeless in the water; in spite of their exact likeness to the creatures they represent, they are utterly unlike anything a trout has learned to respond to. In fact they are like things—small twigs and drifting leaves for instance—that a wise trout has learned not to respond to. The water cannot bend them and turn them and stir them as it can hair and feathers tied to a hook.

Every fly-fisherman has known the experience of catching fish after fish on a fly that has long since been tattered and torn beyond all recognition; often such a fly seems to take fish much better than a new and tidily-dressed specimen of the same pattern. I used to think that the explanation was probably in the immediate conditions, in the day and the way the fish were taking. But I have kept these battered flies sometimes and find that they still do well on another day, in another place, under quite different conditions. The explanation, I think, is that the dressing has become untidy in such a way that the fly works more flexibly and more naturally in the water.

When all these points are added together the conclusion is that there is very little percentage in the precise and careful tying of ordinary wet flies, especially in the larger sizes. It is sensible to attempt imitation, or rather representation; there is no great problem in paying attention to size and color and approximate shape. It is good to have an idea in using a fly, some sort of reasoning and logic to guide its choice, if only for the sake of confidence. But it is far more important to have some roughly accurate conception of just how the fish will be feeding, and on what. Usually, in coastal waters, trout are likely to be interested in drifting organisms—nymphs and larvae swept down by the current, drowned and drifting beetles, ants, caterpillars, bees and other terrestrial creatures. On the whole, the larger forms of such drift are the most likely to produce a response.

It is important then to fish a fly on a slack line, with gut light enough not to interfere with its natural movement, dressed so that its materials respond to the little vagaries of water movement immediately around it.

If the fish are feeding more selectively, on some free-swimming forage fish for instance, flexibility is still an important factor, and it may still be important to fish a slow and drifting fly. But even if they seem to prefer a fly actively worked across or against the current, the character of the fly rather than its color or even its shape is the important thing. It must sink well and fish with a minimum of resistance to the water; in other words, it must have a small and neat head, neatly tied to the leader, its hackle should be soft and flexible, tied to lie back along the hook shank instead of straight out from it, and the wings also must be flexible and tied to lie well down.

Probably I shall tie more stonefly imitations. After all, one has to have some idea of what materials to put on the hook. But once the materials are chosen, my concern is to give them a chance to move and come alive in the water. If an effect of drift is the important thing, such minor distortions as unbalanced wings, untidy bodies, even loosely wrapped hackles, may be an advantage rather than otherwise, though I admit I am conventional enough to try to put the fly together well unless I am deliberately trying to unbalance it.

No materials and no tying are going to change the fact that where the fisherman puts the fly and how he works it are the really important things. But the way a fly is put together and the materials that go into it can make a lot of difference in the way it works. So far as wet flies are concerned, I believe that a fly matched to the fisherman's choice of method is far more likely to be effective, no matter what its pattern, than a fly that imitates appearance without concession to movement.

I hope I haven't said that beautifully tied flies aren't good flies; they usually are, because the conventions of tying developed over the years have been based on repeated practical experience, and are to some extent an essence of it. Really good tied, balanced flies with perfect entry, can be important in greased-line fishing, for instance, especially under extreme low-water conditions in a glassy-surfaced pool. Under most conditions of difficult water and difficult fish, good tying along conventional lines is likely to give the best results. But it is possible to be too much influenced by what is pleasing to the human eye, conditioned by convention, and to overlook possibilities. It is not necessary that the fish be convinced that the fly to which he rises is *Perla*, the stonefly nymph; only that he rise to it and take it faithfully into his jaws. Personally, I doubt if the wet-fly fisherman can ever be sure just what a trout has taken, or mistaken, his fly for. Trout sometimes take drifting duck feathers, not merely into their jaws, but into their stomachs. Fishermen sometimes catch difficult trout, feeding selectively, by offering something in sharp contrast to the favored hatch. Most wild trout are likely to respond to something that looks as though it may be good to eat, and in a stream most things that float or swim or drift with life and freedom are likely to be good to eat. When a reasonably probable fly does not take fish, the fisherman does well to question first where he is putting it, second, what is its movement in, on, against or with the water; if he is satisfied on these points, he can afford to question the pattern or tying of his fly. And he will be wise to wonder at least as strongly whether its general type fits the method he is using, as whether its precise pattern matches what he thinks the fish may be eating.

The Secret Life

A FISHERMAN SPENDS A LOT OF TIME imagining what goes on under the surface of the water, reconstructing from small visible indications where and how fish are lying, what they are doing. Occasionally something happens to give, literally, a deeper insight. Sometimes it confirms the accuracy of the imagination's picture; sometimes it is a big surprise. These insights are not simply a matter of seeing to the bottom of a river and seeing fish moving or resting. They seem rather to have some special quality of revelation that is very satisfying. One feels it, I think, only when convinced that the fish one is watching are entirely unaware that they are watched, and when whatever they are doing is a completely natural part of their existence.

Even this does not say exactly what I mean to say. For once I am almost forced to the admission no self-respecting writer should ever make; this thing, this subtle, simple thing I am trying to express is "beyond words." The trouble is that I often watch fish, knowing they have not seen me, and do not feel the sense of revelation. I cannot remember feeling it when watching spawning or dying salmon, or normally rising trout, or salmon fry concentrated in an eddy. I do not, at these times, feel the complete detachment of the times of revelation, the sense of being, for the moment, a pair of disembodied eyes seeing absolute truth.

I had this feeling one afternoon as I stood hip-deep in crystal water at the mouth of a small stream, a few yards above its drop over a steep, submerged shelf into the lake. I had been up the stream in the hot afternoon and found few fish. As I came towards the mouth I stopped to watch a female merganser with her brood on a sand bar not far away. Because everything was quiet and peaceful, because the light was right and the water brilliantly clear over the gray gravel, I stayed where I was, watching an occasional lazy rise where the stream's current gently creased the still surface of the lake. It seemed to me the rises were coming closer, working up the stream. I looked then into the water and saw a twelve-inch trout swimming slowly, questingly upstream. Five or six feet behind him was another; behind that one yet another. A fifteen-inch fish passed within three or four feet of my waders. I stood rock-still and a smaller fish swam straight toward me and turned from me as calmly as though I were a rock. They were all calm, all dreamily slow and relaxed in the bright water, fish behaving as fish surely do under completely normal circumstances. They were coming up out of the deep water over the gray gravel shelf, to be ready for their evening business of feeding.

I have sometimes had the same feeling of looking in upon a secret life when watching a brown trout cruising an eddy. And I recognized it again when I saw my own Campbell River in extreme low water. Work was being done on the dam at the time and the whole river was shut off except the flow from three 24-inch valves. I took the canoe and poled quietly upstream. I expected to find the fish huddled into unnatural places and this was generally true of the salmon. Humpbacks and tyees for the most part, with a few cohos mixed in, were nearly all closely schooled at the heads and tails of the pools, where the water was still lively. But I found cutthroats and steelheads in the lies where I usually catch them. The steelhead were for the most part hugging the bottom, looking dour and unhappy. The conditions were not natural, but I was seeing into the lives of the fish in a way that is not normally possible. The whole outline of the bottom of every lie was clear, and in many cases I knew for the first time why the fish used it.

In May, when the fry are out and moving downstream, I often go down to the canoe bay to watch them. I like to try to estimate their abundance, differentiate between species, judge their growth, and usually I make a guess at where the trout will be from what I see. The canoe bay is a good place to watch. It is sheltered from the main run of current and has a gently sloping sand beach that is covered by about two feet of water when the river is at normal spring height. The sun strikes from a good angle through most of the day; one can stand well back and everything is clear.

I walked down there one morning last spring and at first could see no life at all. Then a single young spring salmon came swimming into the bay. It was hurt in some way and swimming with a good deal of effort, so I watched it closely. Here, I thought, was the injured fry we try to imitate. He swam slightly tail-heavy, with his head almost pushing against the surface film. Fore and aft his keel sloped, but from side to side it seemed even and steady, and I judged he would be throwing none of the inviting flashes one theorizes about. He swam almost out of the bay, turned back again, out again, back again in wandering circles, and I thought how fortunate he was to be away from the danger of waiting trout. Then another little salmon came swimming into the bay, calmly and competently, obviously in perfect health and quite undamaged. Suddenly a quick shape darted up from the blank sand floor and the little fish was no more. I looked and looked, but could see nothing but sand—and the injured spring salmon swimming awkwardly out near the edge of the current. I had recognized the shape though; it was a second-year steelhead, probably seven or eight inches long.

Other things happened in the canoe bay that morning. More salmon fry came into it, other steelhead yearlings darted up from hiding and seized them. There were at least four, perhaps five, in there. One under the shadow of a stone, three close in under the bank. Occasionally, after seizing a small fish, one would swim calmly in mid-water for a moment or two, then disappear again. The little spring salmon also disappeared, but I had seen no fish take him or attempt to do so.

I went away with an uneasy sense of having seen something I should not have seen; this calm, efficient predation was something I had not suspected of the handsome, silvery migrant steelheads. Of all fish, they are the ones I would most carefully guard and protect, for they are surely my future fishing. It was not strange that they should take young salmon, but I had not supposed they would do so with such patience and such deadly efficiency. Nor had I supposed that a slow, halting fish like the injured spring salmon would survive while healthy fish were taken almost as they showed. I felt I had pried into secrets better left secret.

Two or three days later I was down at the mouth of the river, watching two schools of young salmon holding against the current just inside a big log boom. The school nearest shore was of the year, averaging barely an inch long. The school nearest the raft was of the previous year, handsome smolts averaging perhaps six inches. As I watched I realized that every so often a smolt moved over among the fry and came back with an inch of tiny fish flashing in its jaws. This went on and on, endlessly, apparently without fear or excitement finding its way into either school. It was routine of living, the fingerling salmon of one year preying on the tiny samlets of the next year. Again I had the feeling that I had seen something better unseen and unknown, a shocking fact better left outside the knowledge of a gentle angler. Yet I could not help but be glad. Here, I thought, was a problem of predator control to end such problems. Attack these predators and you are attacking the survivors of the previous year's predation. For once nature seemed to have produced a cycle in which no man could justify intervention.

Boats and Fast Water

THE TWO VISITING ANGLERS DROPPED in in the middle of the afternoon, right at the peak of a good working spell. That is not unusual nor always unwelcome. It isn't too good, though, when they say they are "just putting in time." If the good mood must be broken into, the pen's occasional smooth moment roughened, one likes it to be for something positive, a still better mood to be shared, a still smoother grace of easy communication. These gentlemen were putting in time because they had upset their boat in a swift trout stream and lost most of their gear. It had been a harrowing experience and they described it in full detail.

The stream they had decided to go up is of a good size and with a strong current. It is perfectly clear, running mostly over gravel, without broken rapids or big rocks in that part. It twists and turns a good deal and fallen trees jut out from the banks here and there in that treacherous form of hazard known to rivermen as "sweepers," but the two fishermen had found no special difficulty in running up a fair distance with the outboard. Finally, the boat stuck on a gravel bar in swift current and they decided to turn back. For some reason they chose to stop on the way down, so swung in on the upstream side of a large fallen tree. The rest happened very quickly; the current threw the boat hard against the tree, they rolled it over, clambered on to it, forced it under the log. One of them who could not swim almost drowned. But finally they were both safely on the log with the boat underneath them. After much difficulty, they extricated the boat, bailed it out and continued, fearfully, their way downstream.

The first time this sort of thing happens to one it is a fairly dramatic affair, and I was not surprised that they should want to describe it. But it gradually became apparent that the whole mishap was my fault. I had, it seemed, somewhere suggested that a fisherman might well give this particular stream a trial, thus inciting the innocent and unsuspecting to hazard their lives. Since one cannot, I suppose, assume that every fisherman is a riverman or even a reasonably competent boatman, perhaps I am somewhat at fault. When I think of the seas that can kick up on some of the lakes I have recommended, and the fierce rapids on dozens of streams I have called canoe water or wading water, I feel I am carrying a very heavy load of responsibility. To reduce it, let me clarify things a little.

Fast water, it has always seemed to me, is its own best warning. It turns most men back long before they are approaching the limits of physical safety; this is as it should be, because the moment fear enters, the whole picture is changed. My first rule for anyone not completely familiar with the ways of moving water would be: when you begin to be afraid, go back or get out. My visitors had disregarded this by their own account; they had gone on up the river long after they had felt that the current was frightening.

To make matters worse, they had gone on under power, and that is probably the root of the trouble. If a man knows enough to take a boat upstream under his own power, by pole or oar or paddle, he probably knows enough to handle whatever comes up. But if he has a hundred dollars to invest in an outboard he can get himself into all kinds of places he has no right and no business to be. I don't care much for running up a strange stream with an outboard, though I admit I do it occasionally. But if things begin to look really tough, on stream or lake or salt water, I am very prompt about shutting off the motor and getting out the oars. I have a profound faith, perhaps misplaced, that no sea will ever drown a rowboat if I am rowing it, and I am quite sure that I would rather hit a rock under my own power than under gasoline power.

Having worked themselves by modern invention into a place their own limited skill and knowledge would never otherwise have taken them, my visitors, like uncultured gate-crashers at a formal reception, found themselves surrounded by all sorts of temptations to do the wrong thing. They chose the nearest and laid their boat against the upstream side of a swifter. It isn't an impossible thing to do, though it is next to impossible in a really strong current, but it is such a completely illogical proceeding, so utterly against the plainly visible mechanical laws in operation, that I should never have thought of warning anyone against doing it. Now I know better. Take a boat in on the sheltered side, the down-wind or downstream side of anything you want to land on. What is more, if you have to be told that, and if you can't swim, either stay away from boats or get yourself a guide.

No one can learn to be a riverman from a book. The best riverman I have ever known, or ever expect to know, is Ed Lansdowne, my trapping partner of the Nimpkish days. At sixteen, though he lacked the reasonable caution and sound judgment of the mature riverman and possibly the last ounce or two of strength, Ed was about as good as it is possible to be. I have seen him cross a large, swift, broken river on a small cedar log, wearing running shoes and using a pole. He can pole a canoe, or even a skiff, alone where many good rivermen have to line their boats. He can judge the swing of current round a rock as precisely as a transit measures an angle. He can make quick and accurate decisions for hours on end in a difficult run. He can get out of any trouble he gets into and still have a canoe to take him home—I know this because I have been in troubles with him. He has a sense of balance so perfect that he can stand on the gunwales of a canoe and pole up a bad rapid. And he can handle a standard canoe safely in a sea that keeps thirty- and forty-foot boats tied up in port—again I know this because I have been with him at the time.

Ed learned all this the easy way. He was playing in a canoe when he was so small that his full weight on one gunwale would not upset it. From that he learned, insensibly, how to shift and balance his weight safely as he grew larger. So far as I know he could always swim well. He always lived by a fierce and difficult river. He never developed any fear of water that could tighten or stiffen his movements or confuse his judgment. A full-grown man of unusual physical powers might be able to develop in himself the same degree and quality of skill, but for most of us it is impossible. We simply have to recognize that water can be too tough for us and that fast water must always be treated with a decent measure of respect.

Respect is a very different thing from fear. Fear is a riverman's worst enemy and it is likely to be a greenhorn's only real danger in a river. Few rivers are likely to drown a man who can swim even moderately well except when they are in extreme freshet—and that is not a time when a fisherman goes out. Fast water, even the broken water of rapids, is no more difficult to swim than still water. I have never yet seen a river that had dangerous and mysterious undertows of current when flowing at normal level. Getting bumped against rocks in a rapid is not fatal, nor even very painful so long as one's body is relaxed. The maximum distance one can possibly have to cover in positive swimming effort to reach safety after being upset is half the width of the river. The simple rule is to keep afloat, coast along with the stream, until there is a good opportunity of swimming to the nearest bank; then swim for it, but without haste or anxiety. If you don't make it the chances are that a river's current will sooner or later set you against the bank without your having swum a stroke.

Panic, not rivers, drowns people. And panic usually upsets boats or canoes—the moment of panic that freezes an error instead of righting it. The best way of preventing an upset is to know, by feel, the measure of a boat's stability. A riverman like Ed Lansdowne knows this almost instinctively, because he has grown up with small boats of doubtful stability, but you will notice that he and most other rivermen test a strange boat almost as soon as they step into it by shifting their weight from one side to another. Anyone can do this and learn from it. Ideally, one should take a boat out and test it until it comes to within the smallest possible fraction of upsetting, but this is not always practicable, since that kind of fraction is open to irretrievable miscalculation. The next best thing is to feel it out with reasonable circumspection, learn whether it is quick or slow to roll, easy or awkward to turn, willing to right itself or anxious to keep on going when it starts. In other words, get the feel of it so that any sudden moves

144

will be predictable in effect and the right response will be automatic. In this day of car-top boats, especially the homemade, plywood jobs of faulty design, fishermen venture out in craft that a simple test of this kind would quickly rule out for any sensible man.

A good river boat is a canoe or a skiff or a punt, because these have little or no keel. A canoe is the best of them because it is designed to coast against the current—poling against a stream this point is all-important, as one can take time to find a new grip for the pole without losing ground. Canoes are not especially treacherous, but the standard sixteen-footer with a thirty-three-inch beam can roll very quickly; it is not a boat for a green man in either lake or stream unless he will faithfully keep his weight low by kneeling. A freight canoe, with a forty-five-inch beam, is as safe as a rowboat of comparable size; much safer on a river, and much more useful.

I have found the inflatable rubber boats very safe in running down a stream; in fact, they are almost foolproof, if rather wet in broken water. They bounce off all but the sharpest rocks, ride any wave, handle quickly and draw practically no water. If a snag or sharp rock does hole a rubber boat it remains a safe conveyance, so long as two sides inflate and deflate separately. But they are uncomfortable to fish from and impossible to work against any real strength of current.

Poling a skiff or a canoe against rapids is primarily a matter of using eddies behind rocks. One poles up to a rock, selects another rock, swings to the eddy behind that and so finds a comparatively easy way up through very strong water. It sounds simple but is not, and no amount of explanation will teach as much as half an hour of trial and error.

Coming downstream is much simpler. One only has to maintain steerage way, pick the deepest and fastest channel, and watch for rocks. I usually prefer to take a skiff or a rowboat down sternfirst, rowing against the current. This is very safe as one has plenty of steerage way and plenty of time to see what is ahead. But I admit I often drive a canoe along faster than the current for steerage way because it is much easier to do so. A good canoe rides so light and turns so quickly that one can take more chances. It is also possible to bring a canoe safely down through rapids by dragging a pole on the bottom, to slow the speed and steer.

Rocks show as breaks of white water. If the rock is close to the surface the break will show almost over it. The deeper the rock the farther downstream will be the break. A rock close enough to the surface to do any damage has a tendency to split the current and sweep the boat around it, so it is safest to head just to one side, let the pull take the bow and kick the stern over to follow, or vice versa if one is coming down sternfirst. A rock that shows above the surface has a cushion of water on the upstream side that is almost (but not quite) always enough to keep the bow of a canoe from hitting it.

The safest place in a canoe is kneeling on the bottom, with the knees well apart. This keeps the center of balance low and at the same time gives one a chance to shift weight quickly from side to side; in dangerous water and in moments of doubt this is the position to get to as quickly as possible. But it is also necessary to know when to shift position in a canoe. One man alone, paddling against a wind, hasn't a chance unless he moves up forward of amidships. Running into a beach through heavy surf, the same thing is true; the weight must be forward of amidships to keep the canoe riding straight with the wave. Going out against the surf, the balance of weight must be towards the stern of the canoe.

This is not meant to be an essay on boat-handling, but simply an indication that there is something to the business. No one but a fool would go out to drive an automobile in heavy traffic without some previous instruction; only a fool takes a small boat into rough or swift water without knowing something about it.

On Wading

WADING IS A MINOR ART ALL OF ITS own, with equipment and techniques that mean the difference between comfort and discomfort, safety and danger.

Wading can be one of the most enjoyable parts of fishing. It is good to be in the water without getting wet and cold, and far more enjoyable to fish a good stream or even the edge of a lake from one's feet than from a boat. There are important advantages too; a man wading always knows his whereabouts in relation to a rising fish, and he can cover water at speed of his choosing. Wading, one is more a part of the stream than in any other way, and there is satisfaction and excitement in meeting the challenge of rough water and covering the stream by one's own strength and physical skill.

Modern waders are of many types and it isn't entirely easy to choose among them. For serious wading one can forget the thigh boot; except in a very shallow stream of unusually even depth it is merely an invitation to go out too far and get wet. Waist or breast waders are very little more trouble to wear than thigh boots, and even if one intends to wade only thigh-deep the extra security makes them worthwhile.

There are really only two important parts to a high wader—the material of which the wader itself is made, and the boot. Since the war excellent waders have been made of nylon and other synthetic fabrics; they are light, flexible, tough and probably long-lasting. The only fault I have been able to find with them is that they are colder than waders of the pre-war type, something that is easily countered by wearing slightly heavier clothing under them. The ordinary laminated wader cloth can be just as light and flexible, though, and just as tough; so, unless the synthetic cloths do last longer there is no special gain in them.

Probably the biggest improvement is in the development of the boot-foot wader. An ordinary stocking-foot wader is a lot of trouble. One climbs into it, pulls on heavy wool socks, then brogues or submarines over the socks, all of which takes time. At the end of the day there are wet brogues, wet socks, and the wet waders themselves to be peeled away with cold hands and taken care of. It doesn't matter too much in a full day's fishing, but if one is going out for only an hour or two in the evening it is a lot of trouble. Boot foots are the answer; one pulls them on and is ready to go, kicks them off at the end of the day and is ready to go home. I like this so well that I wear my boot foots most of the time, even though I have two pairs of stocking-foot waders.

My boot foots are made of a five-ply laminated fabric that is extremely light and flexible; it is also cold in cold weather and hot in hot weather, and seems to produce more condensation than conventional fabrics, but it still adds up to a sufficiently comfortable material. The boots that were on the waders when I bought them were felt-soled, of black rubber, quite heavy and with wide, stiff ankles. The first day I wore them I came to a fast run of water that I cross frequently, and suddenly realized that I was afraid to cross it. I studied it carefully and made quite sure that the river was not high enough to cause this reaction, then reluctantly admitted to myself that I was badly out of condition or else old age was catching up with me. I crept across the run, crabwise, with humiliating caution, and saw plainly that the river was not high and that I should have been able to cross without the slightest anxiety. Coming back was the same story. I reached a foot into the heavy water, felt it uncertain, drew back, hesitated, then crept across. It had been a good day's fishing, but I went home in a mood of acute depression, counting the hours left before the old man's home reached out and took over.

Then I thought of the wide, stiff ankles on those heavy, black boots. When I got home I measured the width and found it something over seven inches; a solid slab, seven inches wide by about six high on each foot for the current to tear at. I felt young again at once and sent the waders back to the maker. He fitted a pair of flexible, olive-colored boots that fit neatly over the ankle, and I have worn them for two seasons since without again feeling the onset of senile decline.

This puts the importance of wading boots in its proper light. They should fit comfortably and closely at the ankle. They must not be too heavy, yet they must be stiff enough to give some protection to the feet; a day in a rocky river with boots that are too soft and light can become very uncomfortable. Above all the boots must be properly soled. Rubber soles, except on uniformly even bottom of small gravel or sand or mud, are slippery and bad. Nails, even soft hungarians, are inclined to be treacherous and they wear down or drop out; worst of all, they call for a thick and heavy sole. The only wading sole I have found that is safe and comfortable under nearly all conditions is felt. Fortunately, felt-soled boots are much more easily obtained than they used to be.

I have suggested that a thick, heavy sole is undesirable. In wading a difficult bottom a man learns more of what he is about from the feel of the bottom under his feet than from anything else. A thick, stiff sole destroys all this sense of touch and at the same time destroys any chance the foot may have of conforming to an uneven stance; the unyielding sole rests like a board on one or two high points and gives very little purchase. The high, thick heel commonly fitted to such soles is another danger as it catches and slips as though especially made to do so. I fall rather rarely when I am wading, perhaps once in five years, and then probably through carelessness. Immediately after the war the first pair of wading brogues I could buy were thick-soled and heavy-heeled. I fell twice, very uncomfortably, the first day I wore them. I had the soles cut down to a bare quarter-inch thickness and the heels to half an inch tapering to the instep, then added half-inch felts. I have not fallen in those boots since, though the soles are still less sensitive than I like.

No two rivers present the same problems in wading. A bottom of smooth, round rocks, always associated with heavy current, is the most difficult and uncomfortable of all to wade, though not the most dangerous; it is also the type of stream bottom I mostly fish and probably accounts for my fussiness about wading boots. Sandy rivers, especially when colored as they often are, are far more dangerous; wading is comparatively easy, but the sand washes out into unexpected potholes and hollows, and on a steep slope it can creep away from under one's feet with smooth treachery. Rock slabs and ledges are still more dangerous; it is so easy to slip and keep slipping, and nearly always there is deep water waiting if one does so. Where there are potholes in the slabs, they are sharp-edged, sudden and deep. Loose gravel can be bad, but it is only dangerous in very heavy current and it is not likely then to lie on the lip of deep water. Packed gravel or sand is the best wading of all and in a stream of this type even rubber soles should be safe and comfortable.

A river of big round rocks is the best wading school I know. A man who can keep his feet in it should be safe anywhere. The most important safety rule of wading is: get your feet right down on the bottom and make sure they are solidly placed before you move. As soon as you start to move, you will have only one foot on the ground. If that slips, you will be floating. And if it is insecure it is bound to slip because it is suddenly carrying double the weight and resisting twice the force of current. In a river of big round rocks, one is often tempted to set a foot on the slippery surface of one of them instead of searching around for something more solid. It is always wrong to do so; even when a rock is too big to step over it is better to hold back and feel for a way around it than take a chance. Wading such a river one learns to test and retest footing, to feel always for a solid grip, almost to think with the feet. And that is where all safety in wading lies.

Many of the things I have written about boats in fast water apply equally to wading in fast water. Panic, again, is the most dangerous enemy and panic will drown a man where waders will not and a river need not. Many people believe that it is difficult, if not impossible, to swim in waders. Some believe that air trapped in the waders must inevitably lead to a man floating downstream with his head under water and his feet in the air. Others suppose that the drag of waders is sufficient to pull down any but the strongest swimmer. Neither of these things is true. It is practically impossible to trap any significant amount of air in waders, because the pressure of the water forces all the air out of them; in two or three feet of water one can feel the pressure on one's legs and see the waders flat against them. Any slight amount of air that might be trapped in a sudden fall would be a help rather than a hindrance.

As for waders being a fatal drag, their weight in water is less than out of it. Certainly a man will not swim his fastest in waders but he can swim and he can float, which is all that is needed. The important thing, if one has to swim, is not to waste strength in fighting against the current. Go along with it until there is a suitable landing place, then angle easily across to it. It can never be more than half the width of the river away.

Respect fear—it is a useful natural warning—but do not let it grow into panic. I have noticed many times, both when wading and when poling a canoe, that the same height and flow of water in the same place seems heavier and more difficult in winter than in summer. I once tried to imagine that winter water has some power and strength that summer water has not, but the idea is so obviously ridiculous that even I had to give it up. Winter water can often look worse, because it is roiled and because it reflects a dark sky. In effect it is more formidable because the human body acts and reacts more slowly in the cold of winter and under weight of winter clothing, so the same speed of water is faster in relation to the known speed of one's own muscles. On top of that one is far more concerned about getting dumped off one's feet on a cold winter's day than under the summer sun. These points are worth thinking out, because their sum is that winter water *is* more dangerous than the same flow and depth of summer water. The winter fisherman does well to respect his timidity rather than force himself against it merely because he was able to do in summer the very thing that worries him now.

In wading, as in taking a boat upstream, there is always a sheltering eddy to be found below a big rock or any obstruction. Even a rock six inches or a foot under water can give rest and shelter; the surface water may be surging fiercely over it, but down on the bottom will be slack water. A good big rock can slacken the flow for a hundred yards below it. Even a small rock makes a difference for several feet. The wise fisherman uses these things. He wades upstream, when he must, from rock to rock. And he finds footing in fast water behind a rock when he can; rests in the shelter of a rock when he needs rest.

It is far easier to wade a really fast run at a slight angle downstream than at a slight angle upstream. Sometimes I test a strange place by trying to hold or make way against the current as I cross; if I am forced down I know the place is close to the limit of my strength and must be treated with respect.

Occasionally, in spite of all caution, one must slip and slip badly in fast water. The best hope then is to stride forward after the lost balance, but let the strides

154

be giant and high or you'll trip and be worse off than you were. And if the ultimate happens and the slip becomes a ducking, don't worry too much. Either coast along with the current or, if there is a chance of standing again, turn and face upstream before trying to do so.

I find I slip most often, not dangerously but uncomfortably, when I am wading ashore after fishing out a length of water. I'm careless then, I hurry and I know I'm coming into safer, shallower water. So I forget the rules. And I slip. It's annoying, it's tiring, and it isn't smart. Some day I'll learn and come out as cautiously as I go in.

It is worth thinking out these possibilities and probabilities of wading. Understanding of them makes the difference between comfort and discomfort. It can also make the whole difference between danger and security.

Fishing and the Common Man

ONE OF THE FINEST THINGS ABOUT
the West, about most of the North American continent
for that matter, is that sport is open to everyone. Fishing, especially, is open; there are very few "private"
waters, and many states and provinces have legislation
designed to keep waters from becoming privately
owned. This is as it should be, a pleasant and not too
common recognition of the fact that everyone in a
democratic state has a claim on the yield of its natural
resources.

Anglers and hunters record and establish their claim
by the simple process of buying licenses. And nearly
all of them give at least lip-service to the proposition
that the claim is temporary, renewable annually during the lifetime of the claimant, and carrying with it
an inherent obligation to maintain the resource as a
going concern, unimpaired for the use of future gen-
erations.

Having stated the excellent democratic principle and the admirable intention, thinking then tends to go astray. From somewhere in the glow of democratic exaltation develops the proposition that every man not only has a right to go hunting or fishing, but has the inalienable right to come back with a bag limit; more, there must be a bag limit in every pot and two hanging in every garage.

Bag limits are necessary things, God knows. But they are maximum limits, not minimum and maximum limits all in one as too many anglers, hunters, game commissioners and politically-minded biologists seem to believe. No one has any business fishing on to kill a limit just because the figure twelve or fifteen or twenty has been dangled in front of him like a carrot. No state or province has any business designing its laws to insure that every sportsman, no matter how unskillful, shall have a chance to fill out a limit every time he goes out; there are not and never will be fish enough and game enough for nonsense of that sort. Yet many states and provinces do frame their laws precisely towards this end, and some even plan their game and fish culture towards the same end. It is a policy usually conceived in the shabby hope of wheedling a few votes. In its better moments, it may be based on the woolly misconception that democracy is a great handicap event where virtue's highest reward must be to run level with the field. Nearly always it grows from gross misunderstanding and underestimation of the mythical "common man" or "ordinary guy."

Hunters and fishermen are individuals; there is no

common denominator, no typical gunner or angler, no group large enough, no individual wise enough, or "common" enough to speak for them all. But they are all, by definition, dedicated to one thing, and that is sport. There can be no argument or compromise about this. The meat hunter or meat fisherman, who goes out to fill the pot, is an anachronism. He has no place or part in the present, because there just isn't room for him, and no legislation should give him the slightest consideration.

In sport, method is everything. The more skill the method calls for, the greater its yield of emotional stir and satisfaction, the higher its place must be in a sportsman's scale of values. Trout and salmon fishing, tuna fishing, bone-fishing, pike and muskellunge fishing, all have their ideal methods, clearly and obviously productive of the strongest emotion and the deepest satisfactions. Sportsmen know this and recognize it. Sometimes state and provincial laws recognize it; more often they do not.

In the maritime provinces of Canada salmon fishing is limited to fly only. I have met no fisherman who did not recognize the law as wholly admirable, inescapably right. It insures that every fish hooked or killed yields a maximum of sport, and at the same time goes a very long way towards insuring the future of the sport by reducing the drain on the fish.

The fresh-water fish of the West is the trout. Trout are native to nearly all rivers and streams and lakes west of the Rockies, and have been planted in most of the accessible waters where they were not already present. Trout, above all other fish, are fly-fishermen's fish. Yet·we allow them to be slaughtered by every bait and lure and rigging known to mankind. We encourage the use of salmon eggs, worms, raw beef, crawlers, gang trolls and other devices that insure the minimum of sport and the maximum of killing. And we go on proclaiming our wish to conserve the future of the sport.

I think I must by now have heard all the arguments that attempt to justify this absurdity. From time to time one or other of them has fooled me and I have gone along with it for a while, but I now think them all specious, distorted and ridiculous. Trout, with very few exceptions, should be caught by fly-fishing and no other method. The exceptions are the deeper lakes which have a population of large trout that seldom moves to the surface; in these, trolling should be permitted with simple, single lures, the outside limits of the shoals should be buoyed and the trollers held outside the buoys. Some winter steelhead streams should be opened to artificial baits and lures, fished honestly without floats or bobbers or controllers. The rest of the fishing, summer or winter, stream or lake, should be fly and fly only.

It is not going to happen—immediately. Game commissions will go on stocking lakes and streams with expensive six-inch trout and encouraging "anglers" to come in as quickly as possible and take as many as possible by any and every type of fishhook dabbling or dragging known to man. More and more streams and lakes will be fished out with salmon eggs and worms and gang trolls. Millions upon millions more undersized trout will have their gills and gullets torn out by bait hooks. Thousands more steelheads will turn in lazy confidence to stop the drifting gobs of salmon roe. But in the end the West will understand itself and its resources as the East has done in part. I only wonder, as thousands like me wonder, how much will be left to save when that time comes.

Nearly fifty years ago, Benjamin Kent wrote a wistful hope that the Beaverkill might one day be "reserved for fly-casting only." A year or so later Theodore Gordon, who fished the same stream on occasion, wrote: "Small trout will take a worm all day long and nearly every day, and few recover after having a good-sized bait hook in their throats. . . . We have only a few fish that will rise to the artificial fly, while there are many good game fish for which bait-fishing is the only practical method." And again: "On a good-sized stream one may fish after several fly-fishers without much diminution of sport. I have waited half an hour after nine had passed and then had a very fair day. One or two worm fishers can spoil the sport of many. . . ." There would be a lot more good fishing in New York State today if someone had paid attention to such voices as these.

For myself I cannot care. I shall always find sport enough to keep me happy, and I will go contentedly and hopefully down a pool with my fly behind any number of bait fishermen—provided only that they do eventually move along and not stay lining the pool the whole day through. But I know, as surely as I know *Salmo gairdneri* from *Cottus asper*, that the trout cannot stand it, not even in the abundant waters of the West;

and I know that neither hatcheries, nor biologists, nor all the thought and ingenuity of man can put them back when once they've gone. Far be it from me to identify the "common man" among anglers or to profess to know his thoughts. But if the biologists and game commissioners and politicians would be honest with themselves and him, if they'd tell him to get smart and save his sport by using only its most exacting methods, I believe he'd string along with them. He always has, except when he's been ahead of them.

When Is a Rainbow . . .

SOME TEN OR TWELVE YEARS AGO, IN *The Western Angler*, I ranged myself firmly with those biologists and ichthyologists who feel that the world's trout can be assigned to three species—the brown trout of Europe, the cutthroats and rainbows of North America. Set slightly apart from these are the chars on one side, the Atlantic salmon and the huchen on the other; the Pacific salmon have their own clear grouping, one shade further removed.

I still feel that this is a highly satisfactory arrangement, with as much of the truth of evolution and variation in it as can possibly be recognized by any useful system. And I believe the commonly recognized subspecies among the trouts, three each for the cutthroat and rainbow groups, also reflect, as accurately as is possible within a simple and useful frame of reference, the state of present knowledge of them. But while I should hate to destroy faith in this comprehensible state of affairs, I doubt if it is the final word, especially in regard to the rainbow group.

If it were simply a matter of structural differences, an academic affair of scale counts and ray counts and anatomical proportions, it might not be of great importance to anglers. It is much more than that; it is a matter of life histories and habits and performance in such wide variation that the anatomical differences seem almost insignificant. And therein lies the fisherman's worry.

The principle of scale count differences seems fairly satisfactory up to a point. The larger-scaled fish, with around 130 to 135 scales along the lateral line, are found at the coast—steelheads and coast rainbows. The intermediates, of which the Kamloops is typical and the Shasta perhaps equally so, with scale counts of around 145, are in interior waters. The mountain Kamloops and the Kern river trout with scale counts varying up to 160 or more are at still higher elevations. And the golden trout of Mount Whitney achieves the highest scale counts of all, often between 170 and 180.

So far, so good. It seems an obvious inference that the different scale counts reflect environmental changes in the same species of trout, varying mainly with altitude. When Mottley's experiments showed that scale counts could be varied up or down by varying hatching temperatures, the picture seemed admirably clear and settled. There was just enough to justify subspecific separation as a matter of convenience and on the assumption that persistence of the environmental factors would tend to emphasize the differences. But at the same time it had to be recognized that change of environment would probably modify the differences, and that in similar environment the fish would almost certainly adopt similar habits. The Kamloops trout, for instance, hatched in a coast steelhead stream, might be expected to assume the low scale count of the steelhead and his sea-going habits.

The only remaining confusion in an otherwise pleasantly clear situation was the existence, side by side in the same streams, of the rainbow trout and the steelhead, which apparently had identical scale counts but very different habits. From the angler's point of view this was especially troublesome since the sea-going steelheads attain much greater size and very different superficial appearance, and obviously rate the distinction their common name gives them; yet science could offer no confirmation of this in a separate classification and no ready means of differentiation between a small migratory steelhead and a large resident rainbow. One could only say vaguely, "They're the same fish, of course. Some go to sea and some don't. It's probably hereditary, but . . ."

Obviously this is an uncomfortable state of affairs, a sharp challenge to any argumentative angler or any conscientious biologist. Fortunately, the biologists have begun to do something about it. Between 1938 and 1943, Ferris Neave, of the Fisheries Research Board of Canada, collected and segregated eggs from migratory steelheads and non-migratory rainbows of the Cowichan river system on Vancouver Island, then marked and released the fingerlings. He also checked the scale counts of a good number of wild fish of both types between three and six years old. The results showed small but consistent scale count differences between the types, with the steelheads always giving a slightly higher count than the resident rainbows (three or four scales along the lateral line, five to ten scales in the next line above). It was also quite clear from the movements and later recoveries of the marked fish that the offspring of the steelheads almost invariably went to sea at the expected times, while the offspring of the resident rainbows remained in the river.

There are also Kamloops trout in the Cowichan river system, introduced by the vaguely optimistic efforts of the British Columbia Game Department, an organization that maintains hatcheries and feels it has to put the results somewhere. Neave introduced others and marked them but was able to recover very few. Those that were recovered had the much higher scale count of the normal Kamloops, and there was not the slightest indication that any went to sea to become steelheads or later returned as steelheads.

The importance of these discoveries from a fish-management point of view is obvious. Resident coast rainbows are not a casual by-product of the steelhead runs, nor are the steelheads a simple variation of rainbow habit. The two fish are quite separate stocks and maintain hereditary differences in the same environment; protective measures for one will not necessarily help the other. And the rainbow of higher altitude maintains his hereditary difference when brought down to coastal waters, and apparently does not do nearly so well as the natives.

From the angler's point of view, things are just a shade more confused than they were already. He can no longer call his steelheads and rainbows "the same fish with different habits." They seem to be consistently, though slightly, different fish, with consistently different habits. But the structural differences are so slight that he can still distinguish between them only by their habits. And the difference in habit will not normally be clear to him until the fish are two or three years old.

The explanation, it seems, may well be "glands," as it seems to be in most matters of fish migration. One day the scientists will go to work and find out exactly which glands are the important ones and how they work and perhaps even that their functional peculiarity may be detected by external signs. In the meanwhile the angler must go on as best he can, making his identifications by the logic of where and how the fish is found and perhaps by some indefinable impression of its appearance which echoes experience and seems to tell him, "This is a young steelhead; this is a resident rainbow." Identification of this sort can be remarkably accurate, but not nearly so many men have the necessary measure of experience to be echoed as suppose they have.

I realize that this account does nothing to make things easier. Discovery has gone in the opposite direction to the one I expected, and it now seems that a smaller difference (three or four scales in the lateral line rather than ten or twelve) is both more stable and more significant than it had seemed the larger difference might be. I feel bound to record the discovery because I have previously recorded the other ones. And at the same time I feel bound to make an even more complex confusion by recording my own recent observations of rainbow trout variations in a single stream.

In the two or three miles of the Campbell River below Elk Falls (which fish have never been able to pass) and the salt water, I once supposed there were two important runs of steelheads, one in the winter months, one in May, and an insignificant residue of non-migratory fish, probably chance variants of the migrants. There were some other incidental strays, not too easily explained, but I set little store by these.

Now I can see some pattern and repetition in the strays, I expect something of the rainbows and steelheads in almost every month of the year and I know that either my early observations were faulty or else the proportions of the various runs can change within a relatively short period of time. The major runs seem much as they always were, but the "strays" now seem to have a lot of brothers and sisters.

In December, January and February the true winter run is on. The fish vary in size from five or six pounds to twenty or more. They are probably of two races, one short and thick, one (the more numerous) long and slender. The degree of maturity varies a good deal; a dark fish, full of eggs or milt, may show up in December, and bright fish, apparently less developed, run in during early March. These are variations one expects within a run, and while some of them may be more significant than they seem, one feels fairly comfortable in rating all the fish together as winter steelheads.

During February there may or may not be a sudden invasion of bright little rainbows, obviously from salt water, averaging about 13½ inches in length and varying only by fractions of an inch from the average. They are immature fish, most of them nearly three years old, and they stay in the river only two or three weeks before disappearing as suddenly as they arrived. I have noticed this run three or four times in fifteen years. I may have missed it in some years because I was away at the time or because the river was too high to go fishing. But it does not occur every year. It occurs spasmodically in other nearby streams, and I think it is a sign of a steelhead stream in good healthy production. I feel reasonably sure that the fish themselves are the progeny of the winter run and that they will return later as normal winter fish.

The next run of possible significance comes in late February and early March, a sort of aftermath of the main winter run. The fish are very bright and clean and very small, usually weighing between four and seven pounds.

In May there is a run of fish that one thinks of as rainbows rather than steelheads, though they are obviously from salt water. The normal range is from one to four pounds, with an occasional six-pounder. The fish of two pounds or under are usually immature. Those larger than two or two and a half pounds are mature and seem to spawn within a month of their first appearance. It is rare to catch anything but a kelt of this run after the first week of June.

For many years I believed the Campbell had no true summer run of steelheads. Now I know a small number of big fish (I have caught them from eight to sixteen pounds) comes into the river during June, July and August. There are hardly enough of these fish to be called a run; in a lucky year one might catch five or six between the beginning of July and the end of September, then fish through the next season without firsthand evidence that they are in the river at all. But they are a run, quite possibly a typical summer run, apart from numbers, and I think it is possible their numbers may have increased slightly during the years I have fished the river.

During August and September yet another run of small fish comes into the river. They vary in size from three-quarters of a pound to four pounds or more. Two and a half pounds is a big fish and usually mature; smaller fish are usually immature. My impression is that this run has increased considerably in numbers over the past ten years and is more widely spread through the river. The fish feed much more freely than those of the similar May run and come well to a dry fly. But the time of the year and the low level of the river may have something to do with this.

These add up to six distinct runs of *Salmo gairdneri*. In addition, I have caught a two-pound kelt in August which may or may not have been a remnant of the May run, and several kelts in late November which may or may not have belonged to the furtive summer run. And in June I have caught occasional very handsome rainbow trout in the tidal part of the river. I do not begin to know enough to make sense out of it all, but it is difficult not to suspect that each of these runs is controlled by heredity and that each may have other hereditary peculiarities that will one day be recognized by scientists. I do not think there is much we poor anglers can do about it except keep an open mind. It is important to remember that the rainbow group is highly complex and that the complexities are hereditary and stable rather than environmental and variable. For this reason it is important to pay close attention to both strain and environment in transplanting or stocking attempts; a migratory strain is likely to persist in its efforts to migrate, even when conditions are not favorable; a non-migratory strain will not develop migratory habits simply by being put within easy reach of salt water; a high altitude strain will probably do best at similar altitudes; a strain developed in water of high alkalinity quite possibly needs high alkalinity to thrive. There have been more disappointments in stocking rainbows than with any other fish, and it is quite evident now that most of them were caused by failure to select the strain best suited to the new conditions.

When to call a fish rainbow? I wouldn't know. When he isn't a steelhead, I guess. When he isn't a Kamloops or a mountain Kamloops or a golden trout. When he's caught landlocked in coastal waters. When he weighs less than five pounds in a stream open to salt water. Or maybe just the way we've always done it—when it seems like he's a rainbow.

Leave the Guns at Home

TWO OR THREE YEARS AGO A MAN WENT up to a lake not far from where I live and shot a brood of young ospreys. He explained he had put in a difficult day hunting them, as it was hard to get close. He had believed they were hawks.

This man is a keen hunter and fisherman and has been long enough at the business to be considered something of an expert, yet he spent a day hunting down the beautiful bent-wing ospreys which do not fly like hawks or behave like hawks or look like hawks. No doubt he told himself that he was doing good, killing off an evil predator and saving untold numbers of game birds. But if he cannot tell the difference between an osprey and a hawk, clearly he cannot tell the difference between the harmful and beneficial hawks. It is not only stupid, but illegal to kill the broad-winged hawks in British Columbia. Any man who is making a sincere effort at predator control will at least learn to tell the accipiters and falcons from the broad-wings before he does any shooting; he had better or he may be in trouble. So it is clear that this man, like most hunters and fishermen who are always shooting "predators," was far more concerned to have a target for his rifle than to protect game birds.

A man who has hunted and fished so much must have had pleasure from the sports, but it is difficult to believe that the pleasure of anyone so little observant can have been very great. When I first heard of what he had done, I thought, "It would have been better if he had never been born." What I meant was, "It would have been better if he had never been a hunter." I am sure that the total pleasure of his life's hunting will not equal the pleasure he destroyed—the pleasure of other hunters, other fishermen, other ordinary people who might have watched the three young ospreys he killed.

Hunters have to carry guns and rifles, and inevitably some of them will make targets of creatures that should not be killed. Fishermen don't need to carry guns and they have little or no need to concern themselves with predators that move in the air or on land. Occasionally, herons may be too numerous on small streams that rear a lot of trout or mergansers may become too numerous on larger streams, but these are rare situations, not easily assessed by the ordinary fisherman. A heron, or even a kingfisher, can be an impossible nuisance around hatchery rearing ponds, but this is a special matter and should not suggest wholesale killing of herons or kingfishers. Mink, otters, coons, ospreys, loons, grebes and many other creatures kill fish, but no fisherman in his senses would deny them the right to do so. It is better to see an otter or a loon than to catch half a dozen trout, and it is rarely safe to assume that the harm these creatures do in destroying game fish outweighs the good they do in destroying underwater predators and competitors of game fish.

Bears and bald eagles may become a problem on

western salmon streams at times, but here again it is a question of numbers, and of much greater numbers than one is inclined to think. I once counted over two hundred bald eagles, and knew of fifteen or twenty bears, on a seven-mile length of salmon stream. So far as I know those numbers were normal, yet the salmon were there in tens of thousands as they had always been. In that same year, for the first time, some fifty or sixty seine boats came to work off the mouth of the stream. Five years later the salmon were still coming back, but it was no longer necessary to estimate them by tens of thousands. The eagles were fewer, too; I counted only fifty or sixty. I don't know about the bears, but they also seemed fewer.

Many years ago, on the urging of my grandfather, his keepers, my uncles, almost everyone who had an interest in fish, I used to pursue herons for hours on end across the Dorset water meadows. The herons were extremely wary and I hardly ever caught up with one. The chase was exciting because they were so difficult, and whenever I did manage to get within range I shot without reluctance. But I always felt sorry after I had killed one. They were such beautiful birds, especially on close sight, and I was never strongly convinced of their villainy. In spite of my best efforts, and the efforts of many others along those miles of stream, the herons always remained numerous and so did the trout. Undoubtedly the herons did damage, but I fancy it was rarely serious except when fish were trapped in the irrigation ditches. I have watched herons for many hours, mainly in Pacific Coast waters, since that time and have never seen them take anything but small fish. They prefer the shallow edges of lakes and salt water and the shallow eddies along streams and rivers. They are competent fishermen, patient, swift and accurate when the time comes to strike. Certainly they catch a few small game fish, but they catch far larger numbers of coarse fish, such as bullheads, and much of their food is snakes and frogs. There is not the slightest doubt in my mind that they do much good and only negligible harm in all wild waters.

It would be possible to go down the list of warm-blooded creatures that prey on fish, analyzing the honestly observed habits of each and every one and finding the evil done far exceeded by the good, or at worst so closely balanced that the predator more than pays his way merely by being alive to be seen. It is important to remember that none of the relationships between predator and preyed upon is simple. The little bullhead of Pacific Coast streams, for instance, is a vicious predator. He is also excellent trout food. He is strongly controlled by the American mergansers, and to a lesser extent by herons. The mergansers are controlled by bald eagles and, in the pre-flight stages, by coons, mink and other creatures to such an extent that I watch brood after brood reduced from ten or twelve down to five or six before it is on the wing. In all this man can never be anything but an ignorant interloper, as likely to be working against his own best interests as for them. He had better be content to watch from the outside, except when some obvious overbalance (usually produced by some of his own interferences) needs righting. And the delicate matter of judging whether or not a certain state of balance calls for adjustment is best left to scientists.

Sportsmen who elect to assume responsibility for "controlling" predators seem to me enormously presumptuous. They are saying, in effect, that the natural world is theirs and all that's in it. Because they want the grouse or the pheasant, the hawk or the owl must die; because they want the deer, the cougar must die; because they want the fish, the eagle must die, the merganser must die. Occasionally their needs match those of other people, of farmers perhaps and even naturalists; cougars have no place in the chicken run and crows can be too numerous around a slough where ducks are nesting. But too often they are setting what they believe to be their own interests over those of people who have at least as much right in the natural world. Thousands of people who have never caught a fish or fired a shot find intense pleasure in watching wild creatures. Nearly all the creatures the hunter destroys are enormously satisfying to watch—geese, ducks, grouse, deer and bears, to name only a few of them. The hunter not only reduces their abundance, sometimes to the point of extinction, but he leaves the remainder wild and difficult to approach. When he adds to these offenses by killing off such birds as eagles and hawks and herons, which are spectacular delights to any sensitive traveler, he is extending his interference a long way.

Fortunately, the angler is only a minor offender in these respects. He is, almost by definition, a close observer, and the birds and mammals that follow the creeks and lakes to prey on fish are an integral part of his pleasure. It is obvious that even if he could, by killing them, increase the numbers of fish available to him he would only be reducing the total of his sport. So he can afford to forget guns and traps and go his way with peace in his heart towards all but the rare, rash trout or salmon that dare molest his fly.

On Casting

A FLY-FISHERMAN, TO BE COMFORT-able with his sport, needs to be a pretty good caster. He need not be able to throw a prodigious length of line or to achieve pin-point accuracy; either of these accomplishments may permit him to rise an occasional extra fish, but the chances are the first one will also cause him to pass up fish he might otherwise have found. What he should be is an all-around performer. He should be able to cast effectively into almost any wind; to fish comfortably, from either bank, with trees at his back; to cast far enough to reach fish without exposing himself; to cast accurately enough to cover a given fish; and he should be able to do all these things comfortably, almost without thinking of them, under normal fishing conditions—when wading deep, or poorly balanced or fighting current or cramped for room. No achievement under tournament conditions is worth much to a fisherman unless he can produce something like it under fishing conditions.

Most fishermen learn the overhead cast quite thoroughly, develop from this a casual side-arm and occasionally, under extreme conditions, venture a rather half-hearted roll picked up from watching other fishermen who feel that roll-casting is an unfortunate last resort that may set the fly out a little way.

Having said all this, let me withdraw a little. I am not urging that every fly-fisherman should be conscious of every cast he makes or should be able to give it a name and catalogue number. If a man can fish comfortably, effectively and without undue consciousness of his casting under all conditions he commonly meets with, he has attained the ideal. He had better not interfere with it by bothering to name his casts or remember which one he uses for what purpose. But most fishermen I meet are comfortable only when they have a clear back cast and little or no wind. When they come upon anything more complicated they are likely to call it unfishable.

A professional casting instructor usually lists some ten

or twelve casts for a singlehanded fly rod—overhead, backhand, underhand, roll, spey, steeple, wind, angle, shepherd's crook, and so on. Each one of these is a separate and distinct action, with its own value and its own difficulty. It would be admirable if we all started our fishing lives by conscientiously learning these casts and went on from there to fit them into our fishing. In practice, not one fisherman in a thousand or ten thousand does so; most of us get a little instruction from a friend in how to throw a simple, overhead fly, go on from there and, if we fish enough, develop the others for ourselves.

A really competent fly-fisherman will use most, if not all, of this impressive repertory in the course of a day's fishing on a normally bushed stream. He would probably be surprised if you told him at the end of the day that he had done so, and if you named the casts instead of describing them, he almost certainly would not know what you were talking about. Which is just as well; his pleasure and efficiency are the greater for not knowing. But there are some casts in the repertory that the best of fishermen is not likely to develop instinctively or use without knowing what they are. Anyone who is not ambidextrous is sure, sooner or later, to try a backhand cast; we all learn in the end to lay a cast against a stiff wind; bushes and other obstructions force one to throw underhand and even to produce something like a roll and a steeple. But it would be an exceptional fisherman who developed for himself a spey or double spey. These are two of the most useful casts there are, yet one hardly ever sees them used here in the West—or anywhere else, for that matter, where singlehanded rods are the rule.

Both casts are salmon casts, first developed for double-handed rods; both are immeasurably more comfortable and effective than any simple roll or switch, and both are completely effective with a singlehanded rod though they are smoothest and best with a rod of fairly supple action. A right-handed man will use the spey from a left bank, the double spey from a right bank. An ambidextrous man needs only one of the two casts; he can change hands and use it from either bank.

Both casts use the same principle as that of a simple roll—a loop of line thrown forward to pick fly and leader from the surface and project them to the full extent of the line. The important advantages are that both casts will free a longer length of line more easily than will a simple roll, and they permit a 90-degree change of direction in one cast, while most fishermen cannot change more than twenty to thirty degrees with a roll.

To make a successful spey cast it is necessary, as with a roll, to let the previous cast fish out to the fullest extent of rod and line directly downstream. The rod is then drawn back smoothly and firmly across the fisherman's chest, with the point raised slightly. Fly and leader will riffle along the water and then come free. As they pass the fisherman he drops his rod hand slightly, to pitch them on the water, and in almost the same motion, still smoothly, he sweeps the rod-point back and over to throw the loop of line straight out across the stream. The pull of the loop comes on the fly and leader, breaks them free of the water and catapults them forward.

It is possible to make this cast without pitching the fly on to the water, but the pitch is essential for any real length of cast because the resistance of the water produces the elastic, catapult effect that makes distance. Of the two casts, it is the less satisfactory in my opinion, because it puts a heavier strain on the rod; moderate casts of forty or fifty feet should do no harm, but continual forcing for distance will probably work the cane against its gluing and may spring or break a rod at the first joint. But, even used with circumspection, it is an extremely useful cast, and an indispensable one for any fisherman who wants to fish in comfort under all conditions.

The double spey, made from the right bank, is essentially the simpler cast of the two because the timing is easier. And because the whole operation is smoother it need put no serious strain on the rod. Again, the previous cast must be allowed to fish completely out, to the full extent of rod and line and arm downstream. The rod is brought quite slowly and evenly upstream, across the body, with fly and leader riding the top of the water. Still in the same movement, the rod is brought back over the right shoulder, forming a loop of slack line in the air downstream of rod and rod arm. As the loop forms, the rod is driven forward, the loop follows and the cast goes straight out across the stream.

No cast comes fully to life in straightforward descriptive words, but of all casts this is the smoothest, easiest and most beautiful in fishing a wet fly. It is so comfortable to use, so lazy and pleasant that I often find myself fishing out a reach with it even though the bank behind me is perfectly clear. I use it as a rest from overhead casting, use it to lift a heavy fly safely in a wind, use it when I am worried about a rocky beach or gravel bar behind me, use it to pick up line for a longer, overhead cast. Like the spey, it is at its effortless best with a fairly supple rod and a double taper line. But it also can be made to shoot a multiple taper with a tip action rod.

But no one cast, not even the double spey, will do everything and make completely satisfactory fishing. The essential is to have them all, each one an absorbed fraction of technique, so that the change from one to another is made automatically, without conscious thought, dictated by the conditions of stream and brush and wind and space. And it is surprising how quickly a specialized cast, once learned, can build itself into a fisherman's range and become part of him.

Charles Cotton

ON THE TWENTY-EIGHTH OF APRIL, 1630, Charles Cotton was born, at Beresford Hall in Derbyshire. He died in February of 1687 and was buried at St. James' Church in Piccadilly. He was the first master of fly-fishing to record his knowledge and technique; he was a close friend of Izaak Walton, and his

"Instructions How to Angle for a Trout or. Grayling in a Clear Stream" constitute the second part of *The Compleat Angler*. It is clear that he was expert with the artificial fly as Walton never was, and his claim to be considered the true father of fly-fishing as Walton is of angling in general seems unassailable. What he wrote is clear and practical, and most of it is sound even today. And he wrote ably, with a glow of life and feeling and a deep love of the sport that has seldom been so well-expressed in all the thousands of fishing books written since his time.

Cotton was many things: poet, courtier, soldier, country squire, county official, magistrate or justice, twice husband and five times father. He loved good times and good companions, drank heartily, gambled cheerfully, after the fashion of his times, yet remained a very gentle and sensitive man. He inherited a fine estate but with it a mass of debt from his father's lawsuits. Being generous, open-hearted and convivial, he never managed to reduce the debts, and in the end lost the house in which he was born. He was familiar with duns and creditors of all kinds, as he makes plain in some of his poems; he probably was never free from financial problems, yet he was always happy, always quick to laugh at himself, always beloved.

For a man of so many interests and such a happy-go-lucky character, living in such disordered times, Cotton was a prolific and brilliant writer. Many of his poems are beautiful, intensely felt yet expressed with a simple clarity that surely stems from honesty and lack of pretension:

How calm and quiet a delight
  It is alone
To read, and meditate, and write,
By none offended, nor offending none;
To walk, ride, sit or sleep at one's own ease,
And pleasing a man's self, none other to displease.

He wrote also vigorous burlesques, usually referred to
with mealy-mouthed disfavor by the commentators, and
several treatises, including an expert one on the culture
of trees. But his chief literary fame, apart from his con-
tribution to *The Compleat Angler*, is probably in his
translation of Montaigne's essays, which is still being
issued in new editions. After nearly three hundred years,
his literary monument remains considerable.

Cotton wrote his account of fly-fishing in a short ten
days of March, 1676, to have it ready for Walton's fifth
edition which appeared in April of the same year. The
swiftness of the writing has left an impress of freshness
and immediacy upon the book that still lasts after three
hundred years. It is one of those best and most fortunate
of things, a book thought upon for many years, post-
poned many times, then poured forth in happy urgency
by a skilled writer who has no time for artifice but
remains unbetrayed by his art. It seems likely that Viator
was there at the time, whether or not he was the Venator
of Walton's Angler, and that at least some of the dis-
cussions and incidents recorded grew out of each day's
happenings as the book was written. If not, the illusion
of immediacy still remains perfect and it can only be
that Cotton's enthusiasm and warm personality were
enough to produce it.

I cannot think of a man I would rather have known as a friend than Cotton. He was a writer's writer and a fisherman's fisherman, a true countryman and a lover of mountains; yet he was sophisticated, widely traveled, widely read and full of humor. I cannot detect anywhere about him an atom of meanness or petty jealousy, yet he had an abundance of pride and self-respect and a mass of loyalties that he would defend to the limit. He is the sort of man one chooses and clings to for a hunting or fishing companion year after year and season after season, and finds always richer and more rewarding.

I am sorry he lost Beresford Hall instead of living out his years there, and sorry that the little fishing house by Dove was allowed to fall into disrepair. Yet I do not think he would have let either of these things worry him or affect his good humor, any more than he allowed his debts to bother him, except financially. I like to think that much of the peace of mind that gave him this strength came from the fact that he was a fly-fisherman. Even more, I like to think it was inevitable that a man of such charm and humor, a man so obviously vigorous and active, of such rounded versatility and warm integrity, so bold and yet so gentle, should have been the father of fly-fishing.

Fishermen and Forestry

To be perfectly honest about it, I like trees. I'm prejudiced in favor of them. I'd sooner have a tree in the way of my back cast than a strip of bare bank; I'd rather have a scrub willow or a stunted spruce than no tree at all; if I am to fish a meadow I wish for at least a tree or two along the banks of my river, and for me the quiet gleam of the shaded place on the otherwise open stream is always where the big fish lie—and where my brother anglers may have passed them up.

Deciduous trees are my true love, spaced specimens for preference, maple and birch, ash, beech, alder, oak and all the others, wherever they grow. A fisherman does well to love trees in this way; it is another facet of his pleasure, another symbol of his part and place in the complicated make-up of his world. But it is usually the true forest, the massed evergreens of the long hillsides, that make his sport, the streams he wades, the fish he catches, the creatures they feed on, the quality of water that supports them.

People often ask me why the Campbell River, with its short one and a half miles of spawning water, supports not only the most famous run of big salmon in the world, but noble runs of cutthroats and steelheads and good numbers of the lesser salmons. The answer is not simple. It lies partly in the bottom of heavy rocks and

185

gravel that shifts little even in heaviest flood and so protects the eggs; partly, perhaps, though I am less certain of this, in the aeration of water in the two or three hundred foot drop of Moose Falls, Deer Falls and Elk Falls, only three or four miles from the mouth; partly, I am sure, in the storage of the three great lakes, Buttle, Upper Campbell and Lower Campbell, which have always maintained flow in the driest summers and which hold water temperatures within a reasonable range. But most of all it is in the timber of hundreds of miles of high valleys, which holds back the run-off of snow and rain, prevents washing of the hillsides, and makes a watershed out of what would otherwise be a drainage system.

This timber still stands because Strathcona Park was set aside over forty years ago by the action of a fore-sighted legislature; the loggers have been kept out of these valleys while every other valley on the eastern slope of Vancouver Island was being stripped. So the river flows as it was always meant to flow, and the salmon and trout still come to it.

Forest cover in the high hills is the true protection of angling waters in most parts of the world. On the Pacific Coast it is also the source and protector of the salmon runs, and the destructive logging methods commonly used have probably wiped out more good spawning areas than those two other destroyers, pollution and power dams—though these last two, at the present rate of "progress," may soon catch up. The coho salmon is probably the greatest sufferer. We are all wondering what has become of the great coho runs of only fifteen or twenty years ago. Some of the blame must rest on the commercial fisherman, especially the troller. But the coho is a great creek spawner; in the October rains he ascends even the smallest streams, working over beaver dams and obstructions of all kinds with a reckless determination. He can still go up some of them—in the October rains. But coho fry spend a year in fresh water before migration, and thousands of streams that ran all summer when the timber was standing are now dry for several months in the year. So cohos do not survive to return to them. In many places the forest cover will grow again in time, and I suppose the streams will run again. But not the cohos, unless someone does a lot of expensive transplanting, and perhaps not then.

These are trees in the grand sense, in wholly significant function, providing water storage as reliable as that of the natural underground reservoirs that maintain the English chalk streams. Trees are important, too, in protecting river banks, in shading streams, in breeding and dropping insects to the waiting fish. But a fisherman knows trees intimately, sometimes more intimately than he wants to know them. They reach out restraining limbs and hooks as he tries to walk upstream along the river bank; they haunt his back casts, overhang the lie of his feeding trout, rob him of flies and leaders, and sometimes fish.

It is well to be patient with trees at such times. There are ways of casting effectively with trees at one's shoulder, and every good fly-fisherman should know them for peace of mind as much as for catching fish. It is more likely that the fish is where he is because

187

the limb is overhanging than that the limb has moved in to cover the fish from the angler. And overhanging trees can be very friendly to one's purpose; trout that haunt such protection are likely to feel secure and to rise confidently to the first artificial that floats smoothly over them. A leaf-covered branch is often a perfect supplement to a difficult dry-fly cast; one can throw the fly at the leaves so that it touches and slides off into the water below as naturally as any insect that breathes. Trees and their leaves break up the fisherman's silhouette, make him far less visible than he would be on a bare bank.

So it is well for a fisherman to go along with trees, to like them and make the most of them. Occasionally some special limb or tree makes a fisherman so angry that he cuts it away. It is a losing battle. As likely as not the fish he was hoping for stops rising where he did. And there will always be other trees, other limbs waiting over favorite and difficult places—more than he can ever cut away. It is more profitable to take them as they are and learn to throw under them, over them, around them, between them.

On the whole, trees are kindly enough. I don't know how many trees I touch with my fly for every one I hang up in, but I should judge not less than thirty or forty. When one is young and impatient and resistant to trees, things go less well. Every touch then seems to mean a lost fly, until the empty fly box and the empty pocketbook teach gentleness. Only gentleness is needed; it is really quite hard to hook a fly into a tree if the cast lights gently and the attempted recovery is slow and gentle. Far more often than not the hackles guard the point of the hook and the fly slides away, over leaves and twigs and limbs, to drop smoothly onto the water. More often than not, the pull of the current on the line is enough to do it.

There is the shade tree at lunch time, the tree that makes fuel for the winter fisherman's fire and the summer fisherman's camp, the tree that gives shelter from the sudden rainstorm or a spell of protection from the drive of a gale. One would not wish to be without these, or without the pale green of the sunlit alders in springtime, the shimmer of poplars in summer, the red and gold of maples in the fall. A fisherman's world is all these things, as well as fish and water.

I know a dark cedar tree whose limbs reach far out over the stream, much farther than any tree's limbs should reach, and come down closer to the surface of the stream than any tree's limbs should come, almost touching its summer level. To reach under them at all one must throw backhanded from the far side of the stream, a long cast that travels all the way only a foot or two above the water, then flicks sharply upstream at the cast's end. The water is deep under the limbs, shaded almost black by them, flowing at a good smooth rate. There are always fish there and nearly always one or two are rising. Sometimes I cover the one farthest downstream and hook him. Sometimes I even reach the next one above him and he drops back with my fly, takes it or does not take it. I have not yet reached as far under there as I should like; there is yet another fish, whose rise I have only glimpsed through the limbs themselves. I hope to be back there again next year, and if I am I think I can make it. There was one cast this year that seemed to me far enough, though no fish came to it.

Family Sortie

ONE OF THE LEAST EFFICIENT, AND one of the happiest, ways to go fishing is to take a rod along on the family picnic. It is best to go to a lake or the sea rather than a stream—stream fishing is too attractive and challenging, too likely to separate the family and destroy the easygoing effect.

There are degrees of picnic. One may go out with one or two of the older children and be swept into an intensity of fishing close to frenzy, a determination that moves ever eagerly from place to place in search of better things, caring nothing for weather or mosquitoes while the carefully packed food and drink waits the reluctant pause at dark. Or one may go with the whole family, large and small and in-between, with swimming suits and incidental laughter and still more incidental fishing gear.

We went on such a picnic one hot and windless day
in May, Ann and myself and four children, in varying
ages from fourteen to two and a half, starting toward
one of the many little lakes of the Sayward Forest soon
after the older ones came home from school. I had mentioned Daisy Lake, in answer to searching questions and
just for the sake of having a temporary objective. But I
kept an open mind, in the experienced certainty that
some chance would arise to change the choice.

The start was propitious. As we crossed the dam Alan
saw a bird that was strange to him. We stopped the car
and watched a killdeer running with halting steps across
a wide bank of gravel. There was a motion that we get
out of the car and look for the nest I had carelessly said
was there, but I overruled that and we drove on.

A few miles farther on I watched a raven fly low
across the road and into the bush. I wondered what his
concern might be, and was still wondering as we passed
the place where he had crossed. Alan's voice stopped
us again, urgent this time, a little awed.

"What was *that?* A great big bird with a red head,
sitting on a stump."

"Turkey vulture," I said and slowly backed the car,
hoping that five people who had never seen one before
to know it would see one now. The vulture was co-
operative. He held on his stump, his disreputable, somber
body in round-shouldered concentration, his scarlet
head vivid in the sunlight, until everyone had seen him,
then flapped on great slow wings a few feet farther into
the bush.

We passed a little lake in the timber that seemed attractive to everyone but me, who knew that there was no fish in it larger than two or three inches, came down a hill and passed another lake, wide, still and beautiful.

"Stop or go on?" I asked.

"Go on," they said, and we did, past two more lakes and within sight of a third, long and narrow and with a half-hearted road running alongside it. It was Green Lake and it seemed the place and the time we wanted, so we turned along the jolting road. Almost at once I saw a freshly built beaver dam and slowed the car. It was a fair-sized dam on a small creek that flowed under the road, neat and in excellent repair. The children began to ask questions about it, all at once.

"If you keep quiet," I said, not too hopefully on either count, "we might see one."

Then I noticed ripples spreading out from the fill of the roadway and stopped the car. "One's there," I said.

The beaver seemed not to have heard us. He swam slowly out from under the fill for fifteen or twenty feet. In the middle of his small pool he dived very gently, without any slap of his tail, and swam the rest of the way a foot or so under the water, still in plain sight, until he came to a hole in the far bank. There was a moment of breathless silence, then Alan said: "If we come back and wait, do you think we could see him again?"

I have told him many times, by many beaver dams, that the only way to see beaver is to hide and wait for them to come out. "Yes," I said. "I think you could. He wasn't scared—I don't believe he even knew we were here. And it's a good time of day."

We drove on to a place where grouse hunters had camped the previous fall. There were the remains of two bough beds, the usual scattering of discarded beer and whisky bottles and, down at the lake edge, a little diving platform built of old railroad ties with a narrow plank running out to it from the shore. The children knew at once it was the place they wanted, so I stopped the car and they poured out. It looked like an unpromising spot to start fishing, but at least there were a few white pines left standing to make a shade from the sun, so I knew better than to argue.

Valerie and Mary and Alan went swimming at once. Ann began to sort out the bean pot and the rest of supper with Celie's help. "Aren't you going to fish, Daddy?" the children asked dutifully.

The sun was hot and brilliant, the lake brassy calm except where the swimming disturbed it. "Doesn't look awful good," I said, but put up a rod and began to throw a dry fly among the fallen trees along the shore. A small fish rose to it, missed and rose again. The fly disappeared and I struck, but the fish wasn't there, so I flipped it to him again and let him play with it. He was much too small. There seemed a promising spot a little farther out and to the left of him, so I picked up, lengthened line, changed direction and hung the fly in a tree behind me. From the water Valerie said, "I thought you didn't do that, Daddy."

"I don't," I said. "Not often." But the fly was securely there and I had to climb the tree to save it. I cast again, more carefully, to my chosen spot and rose a good fish at once. He jumped twice and was free.

While the children were still swimming I wandered a little farther along the edge of the lake but could rise only occasional very small fish. There were a few rises far out in the middle of the lake, but nothing at all near shore. Then the osprey came, high up, prospecting. We all watched as he swung down over the rising fish in the middle of the lake, turned back and swept low towards them. He dipped to the still water, touched it and missed his strike. Without haste he flew on big slow wings just above the still water, dipped and missed again several times until at last he came up with a fish.

The children came out of the water; I went back to them and we ate supper. They were all excited at the prospect of watching for the beaver. I said there was no hurry, the later the better. They became temporarily distracted in collecting pine cones, in floating a small log towards the diving platform, in trying to reach a fork someone had dropped under the platform. Celie waddled about with them, balancing along the plank back and forth to the platform. Finally she fell in, face down. For a moment her little red-jeaned backside and legs seemed to float, then they were under with the rest of her. Valerie jumped in with an enormous splash and Celie reappeared, head first, with a bounce that seemed the lake's upthrust from her fall. I took her from Valerie and that was the end of supper.

They all went down then to wait for the beaver. I put on waders and worked for an hour among a fierce tangle of water-logged tree tops between two swampy creeks at the head of the lake. There was not a stir of wind, not a cloud between earth and infinity. Mosquito hawks rode high in the empty sky, the males booming again and again in superb dives and turns whose sound countered the hooting of blue grouse all through the hills. A few trout rose, most of them small, but I hooked two worth keeping and learned some new things about the lake's possibilities, notably that the swampy bottom was solid enough to wade if one cared to take a chance on snagging waders.

Rather than go back the way I had come I walked up along the first creek towards the beaver dam. I saw the children long before they saw me; Valerie sitting cross-legged on the road, a book open on the ground in front of her; Mary and Alan crouching and peering. Their talk was all in whispers and they shushed Celie when she came running along the road from the car. It was quite clear the waiting had not been in vain. It was a pretty place, with young willows and alders growing thickly around the dam and great cascades of dwarf dogwood in full bloom, pouring from every bank and tree stump, so I waited a minute or two longer before I let them see me. Alan saw me first and waved silently. I came out on to the grade and they all told me of it, still talking in urgent whispers:

"Two of them came out, Daddy. They swam around and Celie came and they slapped their tails and went under. We waited some more and they came out again. They climbed right up on the bank and bit the ferns and we saw them for a long time. But Celie would come again; gosh, she was a nuisance."

"You were lucky," I said. "Was there any more?"

"They banged their tails on the water again when

they got back in. You should have heard them. They haven't come back again yet, but they probably will."

"Can we wait longer?" Mary asked. "Until it's dark?"

It was nine-thirty, and the mosquitoes were bad. "It wouldn't do any good," Valerie said. "Celie would never keep quiet."

The night hawks were still booming. "Know what makes that noise?" I asked and made them watch for the dives and listen for the delayed sound. Then we got in the car and drove lazily home, watching for deer along the sides of the road. The deer were there and we saw them.

Essential Simplicity

THE COMPLICATIONS OF A FISHERMAN'S gear, especially a fly-fisherman's, are almost a proverb. Equipment is fun. It is also expensive, which may or may not matter. Much of it is interesting, something that begs to be tried out. Almost as much is of little real value. And an adequate multiplicity can be a real handicap, as most of us know.

Probably there is no way around the temptation to try out this or that new thing, and perhaps it wouldn't be so good if there were. Bait-fishermen, especially, are everlastingly tempted by gadgets that wriggle or wobble or dart or dive or spin in some new way. Newfangled lines are always going to solve all the old problems, and reels full of gadgets are going to solve those the lines don't solve. A fly-fisherman's temptations are less because his problems are obviously less susceptible to mechanical solution. But we are still tempted and we often fall.

This seems a pity because one of the charms of fly-fishing is in its simplicity and cheapness. Almost anyone can afford a fully effective fly-fishing outfit: a twenty-dollar rod, a simple ten-dollar reel, a ten-dollar line, two or three leaders, a few flies—less than fifty dollars will buy all the essentials of good performance. One can spend four or five times the money and get a better outfit, pleasanter to use and more durable perhaps, but it won't be proportionately more effective, may not be at all more effective. It seems a pity to sacrifice this effective simplicity for an expensive confusion of gadgets, but that is what most of us do.

I do not want to put too much emphasis on price. Price is a relative thing, even to two men who have approximately the same income. Personally I have always been convinced that I cannot afford to be a trap-shooter. I know other men, not much wealthier than I am, who spend as much on a few afternoons of trap-shooting as I spend on a year's fishing tackle, yet they tell me they cannot afford a good fly-fishing outfit. The plain truth is that I don't want to shoot traps badly enough to afford it. Any man who wants hard enough to go fly-fishing can and will afford to buy the gear needed.

The real loss in multiplicity of gear comes when it begins to complicate decisions. A man who fishes under widely varying conditions is quite right to have tackle to match them. But when he finds himself worrying about which rod, which line, which set of flies to take out with him for a day's fishing, he probably has too much. When he gets to the river and wishes he had brought the other rod, the other line, the other set of flies, he undoubtedly has too much. Fishing is meant to be pleasant relaxation, and not a vehicle of self-reproach.

I suppose we sin most in accumulation of flies, and there put upon ourselves the most onerous decisions. I have suggested that there are ways of simplifying this difficulty, my own way of thinking of flies in types rather than patterns, and other ways that other differently constituted individuals undoubtedly work out for themselves. One distressing thing about a multiplicity of flies, beautifully sorted into elegant boxes, is that a fisherman can literally burden himself with the weight of them. My suggestion here again is that one should be guided by types. It is well to slip a few dry flies into a box of wet flies, a few wet flies into a box of dries. By all means have a box of winter steelhead flies, of brown trout specials, of tidal water infallibles, but include in each a sparse selection of other types. Then, when the time comes to go fishing, select the *one* box that fits the day's purpose, secure in the knowledge that it covers also the other possibilities. And never have regrets for the rod, the line or the fly left at home; the chances are it wouldn't have worked that special miracle it seemed designed for, anyway.

I won't go into the complications of clothing—rain

clothing or cold weather clothing, fishing vests, fishing bags, baskets and creels, or even waders—except to say that one tested favorite is worth a dozen alternatives. A very light, genuinely waterproof jacket that fits easily into pocket or creel is worth its weight in gold, and probably costs that much. But it can make a power of difference to comfort on a changeable day. Much of the rest is habit. The old coat, the old fishing vest, with the familiar pockets that fit habitual uses, will give more solid ease and comfort than all the advertiser's darlings.

Fly-fishing is a matter of a few feathers on a hook. The rest of it is supplementary, though some of it is essential. A leader fine enough to deceive the fish, a line heavy enough to carry out the fly, a rod to drive the line, a reel that will store line, let it out, bring it back in. It is well to hold this conception in mind and to depart from it as little as possible. Its normal extension includes a fly box, a leader box, a bag to put the fish in, a simple landing net or gaff, and very little more. The rest should be performance, not equipment.

In simplicity one travels light—no small advantage this. In simplicity one avoids the everlasting confusion as to cause and effect. Trout have been caught for hundreds of years, and caught skillfully, delicately, satisfyingly, without a fraction of the modern aids of fly-fishing. Trout may be more difficult than they were, though I doubt it, and I am quite sure that such modern improvements as the split-cane rod, the double-tapered line, gut and nylon leaders are more than enough to compensate. The problem is what it always was: to place the feathered hook where the trout is in such a way that he is persuaded to take it into his mouth. When persuasion fails it is more profitable to be free to examine one's stream craft and technique—where the fish was sought, how approached, where the fly fell, how it fished—than to wonder what might have been achieved with the other rod or with fly in the box left at home.

Don't You Ever Get Tired?

ANN, WHO IS MY WIFE, AND USUALLY most forbearing about my quaint interest in fish and fishing, asked suddenly the other day, "Don't you ever get tired, going back to the same old places every year and fishing the same old way?"

There are many answers to the question, as Ann well knows. But none of them is as important as the question that arises from the question: "What is fishing all about?"

At the time the first question was asked we were idly fishing a shoal in a big lake. I had just previously fished a creek mouth, and fished it very badly, under the irritating eyes of an unwelcome audience. There were fish rising there, mostly small rainbows. It was midday and they rose lazily, almost invariably short to anything I offered. I noticed they were rising just as lazily and almost as ineffectively to the naturals, but I persisted, missed fish after fish, hit my fly against the rod and broke it off on a back cast, broke another fly off in a twelve-inch fish because I hadn't tied the knot properly, hooked, landed and returned two or three small fish that I didn't miss on the strike. This last to the genuine, but still aggravating, applause of the audience. It was a relief at last to pull out and go down the lake to the isolated shoal, even though the fish were still rising lazily at the creek mouth and I hadn't found the combination to overcome their noonday unconcern.

Nothing was rising over the shoal. But there was a light breeze to drift the boat across it and I cast a dry fly with honest concentration as we went. Suddenly a fifteen-inch fish jumped right out of the water beside the fly. He came down on it, I felt him for a moment and he was gone. So I cast again, rose the same fish or another like him, pricked him hard and lost him. Twice more within the next five minutes the same thing happened. I commented vigorously. That was when Ann asked the question.

In point of fact, the shoal we were fishing was one I had fished only once or twice before. It is a wide bay in a big lake, lying just around the corner from the mouth of a smallish creek. It shelves gradually out from shore to a depth of twenty feet or so in a hundred yards. There are always a few fish of a pound or a pound and a quarter lying there and willing to rise to an artificial that falls near enough. Occasionally the whole bay can boil with rising fish, literally thousands of them, feeding on some unusual hatch, but one can go there a hundred times and not find this.

As the boat drifted and I cast my fly over the blank water, I wondered just what it was I was looking for.

It was a nice day and this had seemed a convenient place to stop and fish for a while on the way down the lake. It ought to yield two or three fish of fourteen or fifteen inches. Up to this point you could pretty well call it. Had called it, I thought, as a fifteen-inch fish rose to me and I hooked him solidly. It had been a pretty, rolling rise, sudden and utterly unexpected, almost as the fly touched the water after fifty or sixty completely unrewarded casts. That was something. One could not tell where they would take, or how, and the solid rise of a good fish to a floating fly is something that never stales. But the shoal has more than that. It is a pretty place to be, and it is a promising place. There are always fish there and occasionally those hordes of fish. Why? For miles on either side of the shoal the lake shores drop steeply into deep water. There are fish scattered along them, and fish scattered out in the deep water across the lake—on a still evening or in the glass calm of early morning one can see them rising. Does something suddenly stir them from miles around to come into the shoal? Or are they always nearby, just under the drop-off at the mouth of the bay?

I netted my fish, killed him, measured him and cast again. Another fish came at once, took the fly perfectly, going away from me. Somehow I missed the strike, touched him hard but never held him. That was unusual, a check to experience, because my mind had said as I tightened that the rise was good and he was mine.

But there is something else about the shoal, about the whole big lake and all its shoals and stream mouths. I have fished them now, always with a fly, for fifteen years. I have never caught a trout there larger than two pounds and very few of those. Yet there are a lot of very big fish in the lake, fish of four and five and six pounds. I know, because I have watched them on calm sunny days cruising the edge of the drop-off, deep down, unconcerned with the surface, yet thick, solid, handsome fish. And I have seen a few of them caught by trollers and bait fishermen, beautiful greenish-brown cutthroats, handsomely marked and of almost frightening proportions. They must stray occasionally, must come up sometimes from their everlasting search for bullheads to lie within reach of an artificial fly's temptation.

Perhaps they never do. Perhaps I shall never see the enormous shape rise slowly up and up through the clear water over the light bottom of the shoal, or the shiny neb break the still surface to take my fly. It doesn't matter much because I believe it can happen—I expect it to happen. And the shoal is as good a place to expect it as any I know.

One fishes for the expected and the unexpected and learns from both. If fish or rivers or lakes were even nearly predictable, a good part of the sport would be gone. But fish live where men don't, in ways of which men have only a rudimentary understanding. By the pleasant, haphazard means of going fishing one learns and unlearns about them constantly. Occasionally, understanding seems almost within reach; in the next moment something has happened to put it as far away as ever. For twenty years I have fished the two-mile length of the Campbell below the falls, and now I know more questions to ask myself about the river and its fish than I could have dreamed of twenty or even ten years ago.

Yet the things one does know are immensely precious and it becomes immensely important to go out year after year, in the same times and the same places, to retest the knowledge, to try to recapture the sensations, to find differences and exceptions.

I suppose it is silly to be so concerned about the response of a fish to a bundle of hair and feathers tied on a hook. Yet that is what remains exciting. The stop, the pull, the slash, the dimpling rise, the surging, savage boil, all those are sensations so powerful that hand and arm and eye write them indelibly on the mind, and they remain there, on recall at any time. Light on the water, break of wave, sweep of current, mountains at one's back, the cry of a loon, beaver or otter swimming; the drive of a gale, the peace of a summer's day or the silence of winter's cold; warmth of friendship, a mind that thinks in tune with one's own—all these things can gild the moment, add to it, exalt it. But the end of it all, the reason one goes back and back, the logic of the illogical obsession, is simply the unpredictable way of a fish with a fly.

Garden Party Day

IT IS FASHIONABLE TO CALL ANY OCCU-pation that does not contribute in some dull way to the world's material wealth an "escape." It is a ridiculous fashion, as little connected with reality as acute insanity. Many people spend their lives in work that is materially quite unproductive, yet has a closer touch with reality than any simple, straightforward job where sweat waters yield. I remember a sympathetic left-wing friend once wondering what would become of me in his revolution. "A writer," he said musingly. "Well, I suppose a writer is a producer in some sort of way. Or is he?"

Feeling the liquidation squad close behind me, I said boldly, "Producer, hell. A writer's a natural resource." He puzzled over that one for a long time and never did come up with an answer.

This has slipped a long way from my point. What I started out to say was that it is fashionable to consider most forms of recreation "escape." Perhaps some of them are. Habitual and heavy drinking may be, several forms of gambling seem to be, intense preoccupation as a spectator with spectator sports may be, just as regular attendance at shallow movies undoubtedly is. But I think the list had better close just about there, and close with the admission that the "escape" generality can have plenty of exceptions. Strange as it may seem, lots of people do things because they just plain like to do them; they get a kick out of doing them, and don't give a damn whether the thing they are doing is productive or unproductive, whether it provides an escape from reality or a highway to reality.

Reality for any properly constituted man in a properly constituted society can never consist solely in materially productive work. A balanced and rounded man who is really living a life instead of enduring it will have many interests beside his work, and they will all be part of his reality. Sports like hunting and fishing, actively and positively followed, are an important and integral part of living for many men. They are not escape from problems or work or reality, but are complementary to the more ordinary, and often less exacting, routines of living, giving substance and meaning and rounded form to a life that would otherwise be a monotonous passage through some seventy years of the world's history.

Now that I've made all this good argument, I can afford to admit that at least once a year I do use fishing as a means of escape. Early in June, when the peonies and iris are blooming, there is nearly always a garden function at our house, a party or bazaar or something of that sort. So I wander up the river for the afternoon.

This first week or so of June is on the edge of the year's passing from spring to summer; in some years it is still spring, in some it feels like summer, but there is always the freshness and light of spring still in the green of leaf, in the whole promise of the earth, in the movement and song of the birds and in the forceful river itself—in the river most of all.

It is not a time I usually go up the river; that is why I admit the escape motive. The snow run-off is likely to be at its height then, the migrant salmon fry have gone off to salt water and most of the cutthroats have gone with them, and the May run of small steelheads has spawned. So there is comparatively little to look for and only a limited chance of reaching that little. But there is an invitation in this very lack of promise. There may be something there one has not found in other years. Some run or reach or glide that never holds fish in ordinary water may hold them in high water.

I went up on garden-party day this year, as usual. The river was very high, so I went into the water at the crooked maple, a lovely tree that reaches out over the river and sweeps upward in a mass of leaves that always hides a robin's nest. It is a good place to go in, because one can ease down and across with the current to the bar between the islands when it would be very hard, if not impossible, to work up there in the usual way. I made it all right, worked well out along the bar and fished the heavy water carefully without finding a thing. It did not matter. The heavy water was splendid in the sunlight. Bandtail pigeons flew back and forth across the river and twice a brilliant sapsucker, scarlet and yellow and black and white, passed within a few feet of me. The big old beaver was working at the mouth of the swamp across from me and a turkey buzzard circled high over the dead tops of the trees above him. I went on down and still found nothing until I came to the pool where the little river comes in.

I should have known better than to fish the mouth of the little river in that high water. It is a giant's confusion of enormous rocks and strong currents and unexpectedly deep holes. It is not dangerous, but it is thoroughly awkward and an excellent place to get wet. It also seemed to me, at that particular time, an excellent place to find a fish. So I waded in, in cheerful confidence, still admiring the day and the water and my whole venture into the imponderables of June when, but for the garden party, I should ·have been solemnly sitting at my desk and writing another book or another story or some unnecessary and quite unproductive letter.

I recognized the little cedar log as a hazard quite early in the proceedings. It was perched and balanced on the largest rock of them all, seeming a little insecure with the rough water lapping at its lower side, and obviously in the way of water I wanted to fish. It was a nice little log, about twenty feet long and a foot in diameter. But I noticed a fair number of shaggy knots along its otherwise smooth and even surface.

I swept the fly along one side of the log and nothing came out at it, bounced it in the cushion of water above the big rock and drew it up to me, searched the other side of the log, still without result, and moved on. The next cast was easy; I recovered it from somewhere just below the log's outside end. But from there down I had to fish over the log to cover the water that should be covered. I warned myself that I was being foolish, that there was no real reason to expect a fish when there were none elsewhere; but I promised myself I would just give the thing a quick chance and take no risk of becoming seriously involved.

The first two or three casts worked out quite well. I recovered nicely over the top of the log without touching it. I moved down a little farther, into water a little deeper and a little stronger. The recovery should have been easier, but the line drowned in the eddy behind the rock, I picked up a shade too quickly, and the log had the fly.

I was still resolved to be careful. I would break without hesitation if necessary. But first it was worth moving a little, to throw a loop of line downstream and hope its pull would free the fly. I moved into still deeper and faster water. But the loop did its work and freed the fly.

The next cast hooked the fish. He showed suddenly, about thirty feet below the log, swimming close to the surface directly behind the fly, a bright and silvery fish of three or four pounds. I slacked the fly and he had it at once, turned with it and ran across the mouth of the smaller stream, among the big rocks. I brought him back into the eddy below the big rock that held the log.

It occurred to me then that I would have to go down to the log or past it to land him. My admirable caution began to fade a little. I still admitted the log was precariously placed and the water near it would be uncomfortably fast and deep. But it shouldn't be too hard to reach over it with the landing net and bring the fish safely up in the eddy.

I let the fish rest and began to work down. It was fast and deep. The rocks on the bottom were large and slippery and I had to pay close attention to my footing. Then I felt a pull on the rod top, looked down and saw the line drawn tightly around the log. It took me a moment or two to understand what had happened; the fish had swum upstream, under the log and on somewhere into the heavy water behind me. I stumbled the last two or three steps towards the log, reached out a hand to steady myself, touched the log and started it rolling off its rock back towards me. I plunged away from it, slipped, filled my waders, found balance again and saw the log spinning like a buzz saw. Fortunately the reel ran freely, but my fly line was wrapped round and round the log, tangled in a dozen of the protruding knots; the rod point was dangerously bent and the log threatened at any moment to slide past the rock and away downstream. What had happened to the fish I did not know or greatly care. The immediate problem was to save a ten-dollar fly line and a precious rod. It took me fifteen or twenty minutes to do it, holding the log, rolling it back and forth, almost losing it, catching it again, working down with it into faster and deeper water all the time. In the end I came out with rod, reel, line, leader and fly. But no fish.

I stripped off the waders and most of my clothes and lay in the sun for an hour, partly because I knew the garden party would not yet be over, partly because I wanted to reduce the evidence of the nature of my "escape." If one has spent an afternoon away from the cares of the world one should at least return from it with an air of composure and relaxation.

Fishing and Milkmaids

THE PACIFIC COAST IS THE LAND OF the mountain torrent. Only in the great valleys of the enormous rivers do we have quiet flowing water, and even here the quietness is not for long nor is it without a fierce strength. Most of the streams we fish are rushing and rock-broken, alternations of deep pools and white water rapids, sometimes shadowed by canyons of solid rock, sometimes spreading among built-up gravel bars. They have their own quietness, but it is the quietness of accustomed sound; their own peace, but it is the peace of energy unbounded, leaping its free way through sunlight and shade to the never-distant seas.

No fisherman could ask for better things than these to live with. They are trout and salmon waters beyond all other waters of the earth. They are beautiful, they are clean and clear, they are full of infinite variety. Yet they are never pastoral. Even when they flow among rich farms, in smooth valleys stripped of timber, they hold to their own quality of hurry and rawness, with the urgency of the mountains still close behind them; one feels it in the unexpected strength of the water against one's legs; recognizes it again in the rounded rocks of the bottom or the heavy sand deposit at the edge of an eddy. One can imagine Charles Cotton, the fly-fisherman of Dovedale, finding accustomed delight in such waters, accepting them without surprise and making them quickly his own. That is as it should be because Cotton, not Walton, is the true father of fly-fishing, the first of us all to express love and understanding of trout and trout waters. Yet we are also Waltonians, lovers and brethren of the angle; the quiet ways, flowering meadows, the milkmaid's song, are part of our inheritance, whether or not we have known them.

No man loves the felt-soled boot and breast-high wader more than I do, no man throws a fly at leaping current waves with greater pleasure or keener expectation. Yet I remember well the easy, unhampered walking through the meadows, the calm of resting under a shade tree to watch a long, quiet reach of gliding water, the rhythmic, tearing sound of cropped grass as some rich dairy herd fed along the river's banks. And even more than these, the chance meetings with country people about their country affairs—hedgers and ditchers, herdsmen and shepherds, keepers and millers and farmers, the exchanges of tobacco and information, acceptance and acknowledgment of each other's business there in the meadows.

Here, these things have their dimly recognizable counterpart; the trapper in his cabin on lonely lake or stream fork, the occasional game warden or prospector. We accept the deer coming down to drink, the bear seeking berries, the beaver swimming, in place of the slow-stepping Red Devons, the gleaming Jerseys or the block-bodied Shorthorns. They make a wilder scene, more exciting and unpredictable, essentially different. One may prefer it, as I do, but the other remains a part of angling, a part of fly-fishing.

Occasionally one finds a length of stream, a setting that creates the same quiet mood of wandering, easy purpose. I know a half-mile of stream below a rocky fall that ends a steep-walled canyon. The stream bed is coarse gravel, gray limestone made palely brilliant by a mixing of white quartz, and changes yearly in the violence of spring and autumn floods. The water is clear, with the relentless, magnifying clearness of the mountains that seems to make a richer world of seeing and tempts one to wade the unwadeable. When I go there in the heat of August I become suddenly lost between high solid walls of cedar and fir and alder. What wind there is is high above the tree-tops; down there on the stream there is only the lazy summer hum of insects, the float of mayflies on the blue-green surface of the gliding water, the occasional quiet rise of a trout at the point of a sweeper far under overhanging cedar limbs or tight against the log along the far bank.

With eyes tight shut one would know it from the other, of course—the coldness of the forty-degree mountain water against one's legs, scent of cedar and fir instead of hay and meadow flowers, croak of raven, chatter of hawk, laughter of orange-shafted flicker or belted kingfisher echoing against the forest walls. But wading upstream in the sunlight, with four or five good rising fish marked ahead, the memory is touched, the other scene recalled. A cast to a rise under hanging bushes, the float of the fly close along them, the quiet rise, the cutthroat that runs upstream, runs twice or thrice again, then comes almost quietly to the net—all these things build on the memory and hold the mood. The next fish is far, too far, under dark overhanging limbs. The cast shoots well, close above the water, the fly carries almost far enough. It drifts past the rise, untouched, begins to drag, and the fish has it. He runs wildly downstream, jumping and jumping, and the power of the gliding, ice-cold current has sudden meaning. A chalk stream was never like this, nor even a sea-trout river.

From a literary point of view, it is far too easy to call similarities or contrasts—the two things can be made to seem as like or unlike as one wishes. Compare the quick little harlequin female, diving below the falls where she has her nest on some rock ledge, to the white, waddling procession of barnyard ducks; compare the beaver to the water vole, the bear track to the cow track, the thunder of mountain water to the chuckle of valley water, and the contrast is complete. Call the two kingfishers similar, match the Audubon warbler to the yellow wagtail, notice that the water ousels are alike, that mayflies float and trout rise in both places, and the differences almost disappear. It is all a matter of a fisherman's mood, whether it picks upon the similarities and recognizes their echo, or watches the sharp differences and chooses to delight in them.

I know I want one day to go back and make the comparison from the other side of the Atlantic Ocean. From time to time I think of a certain place, a certain season, almost a certain fish, as being best for the experiment. At the moment I think of a sweeping bend in a small south country stream. On my own bank, on the inside of the curve, is a withy bed and an old man is cutting and splitting the willows and tying them in bundles; later they will become sheep hurdles. I have spoken with the old man, heard his account of a mallard with a great brood of young ones hatched off in the withy bed this season, followed the pointing of his thick finger to see where a big trout was rising last evening— but now is not. The old man has gone back to his work, and I to mine.

The current rides swiftly round the bend. On the far side of the stream are two great tangled blackberry bushes; between them the bank has been cut away into a little bay, and an eddy forms there. The surface of the eddy is a scum of sticks and broken river weed and river foam packed into a solid mass, and the current slips swiftly along it, carrying intermittently small, pale duns. A trout's nose lifts to intercept them, making almost imperceptible marks on the surface, each one instantly distorted and washed away by the current.

One is conscious of the gleaming half-inch of neb that breaks the surface, rather than of the rise dimple.

I have a No. 16 pale watery, on 4x gut. The cast is one I have made many times before, successfully, twenty or twenty-five years ago. The line must fall slack across the stream, the belly slightly upstream; the fly must touch down a foot short of the overhang of the upstream bramble and three or four inches out from the scum of the eddy. The current will sweep it in, almost as it lands, and over the dimpling trout. I wonder, first, if I can still do it; second, what shall I think as I try? How like, or how unlike?

The Depth of the Wood

I FEEL AT EASE WITH FISHING, EVEN with writing about it, because I have been through and come out on the other side. I do not mean by this that I know all the answers, or even a major fraction of them. Rather, it is as though I had found my way clear through a deep and beautiful wood, from open daylight to open daylight, and knowing the way, were free to turn back into the wood and search in peace and leisure for all its beauties. In reaching the other side I have found nothing that cannot be found without going clear through, except that the wood has a limit in at least one direction, that it is good all through and that nothing beyond seems better.

More concretely, I feel I know the range of possibilities and satisfactions that fishing can offer; that I know what makes the sport worthwhile for me and what is merely surface stuff of no urgent value.

The first thing I do not want is to excel as a fisherman, to catch many fish or fish of record size, for instance, or to be perpetually on trial as an "expert." I want to catch fish, of course, and I like to fish with the chance of finding big fish, even record fish, but I am not concerned with records—only with fish that will set problems worth my solving. I want to be a good enough fisherman to have a chance of solving the problems such fish present, and I want to be good enough to be comfortable, to be thoroughly interested, to know all the time, or almost all the time, what I am about.

I no longer feel any fierce compulsion to try every kind of fishing. There are many kinds I have not tried and if things work out that way I should like to try at least some of them. If not, well and good; I do not think I shall miss any spectacular surprises, because I feel I have fished enough to know the essential substance of even the untried ways; and I am reasonably certain that I should not find in them any intensity of experience that cannot come equally well from the fishing ways I do know.

The main reason for this relaxed attitude is that I feel the passage through the wood has taught me to recognize the fullest implications, the whole and true values of the things that happen in my own way of fishing. I have not seen everything that is to be seen, or felt everything that is to be felt; far from it. But I know that worthwhile things will happen to me in the course of every day's fishing and that when they do happen I shall know enough to understand them and draw the utmost pleasure from them.

Realizing this, it is enough simply to go fishing. The rest is bound to follow. I no longer want the ultimate perfection in tackle—I want good tackle that works smoothly and well, doing its job without inflicting irritations and petty distractions upon me. But I am not interested in new gadgets that will enable me to cast to great distances, or reels that do automatically half a dozen things I can do for myself without stopping to think, or flies that so show their light through the water that no fish can resist them. I have known all these things, or others much like them, and I know they will work no miracles for me or for anyone else. And if they did work miracles, what would be gained? The object is to go fishing, to enjoy going fishing and perhaps to perform well enough to solve a few problems and catch a few fish. An assortment of miracles achieved by gadgets out of *Popular Mechanics* would be enough to upset the whole business.

I no longer want ideal conditions of weather and water, though I look for both within reason. But a bright and pretty day, a day when one is free to go, is the day to go fishing, even if the fish do not think so. I no longer search for a great abundance of fish; it is enough to know that there are a few around, of worthy size and reasonably likely to respond to the best I can do. Even less than that is enough; it is enough, sometimes, not to know that there are no fish in the river

So long as one has the conviction that there ought to be fish around somewhere, one can have a very pleasant time looking for them.

I suppose the way to all this is through the very things whose worth I am denying, through perfect tackle and miraculous gadgets, abundance of fish, variety of conditions and spectacular triumphs. So long as these things, or the pursuit of them, remain satisfying, clearly they must have worth. My point is only that they are not likely to remain satisfying, and that even while they do so they are obstacles in the way of more real satisfactions. One passes them on the way through the wood, notices them because they stand out so plainly along the path, for a while supposes them to be the true substance and character of the wood. But the wood's reality is far more subtle and complex, discoverable only as one's eyes become accustomed to its light and adjust themselves to search inward.

I could not say exactly what it is I expect from a day's fishing now as I start out, only that it is something very much more than fish, something more even than good fishing. It can be in almost anything about a day on the water, in combinations of things or in successions of things or in single, isolated things. The only certainty is that it will be there if one is looking for it. It has much to do with reflected experience, with subtle variations of experience and with the sport's whole background. Its quality certainly depends on the mind's readiness to fit each new happening into the framework of its own knowledge.

I shall never be able to subdue the excitement of fishing new water, but I cannot tire of fishing old water that has yielded good sport, or stop expecting great things of it. I nearly always search hard for fish when I go out and I think I try as eagerly as I ever did to solve any and every problem that comes up. Some problems, such as that of persuading tyee salmon to take a fly in fresh water, I love because, for me, they remain insoluble though not without hope of solution; others, such as the discovery of new lies where winter steelhead will take my fly, I love because I do occasionally solve them yet they move always ahead of me, problems still; others again, such as the discovery that trout will often take a large fly amidst a hatch of small ones, I love because they have taught me things about fish that remain part of my working knowledge, into which I can fit other things.

These are fishing pleasures. But there are many besides them, less essential to the sport but no less a part of it. It is keenest pleasure to know how to watch fish and understand a little of what they are about, to know something of water and its ways, something of birds and other creatures that move near water, as well as things that grow near water. Above all it is pleasure, and the sport's essence, to fish with other men who are receptive to all these things and perhaps other things one has not yet found for oneself. I like to fish alone, and often do. But my happiest fishing days have been with friends, some of them experts, some of them beginners, but all men who found strong pleasure simply in being out on the water.

This book has no message, and heaven forbid that

I should wish one on it at this late stage. But it has in large measure grown from the intimate, relaxed exploration of the wood that seems to me the highest satisfaction this most sophisticated of sports can offer. Its intention is only to share pleasure as fishermen share a joke or a fly or a flask beside a stream. The writing of it has been pleasure and in itself often a deeper exploration of the hidden places of the wood. I know well that there are other ways through, from daylight to daylight, than my own, other treasures to search for than those I seek. One of the charms of the sport is its infinite complexity, its scope for men of diverse minds and bodies and skills. The pattern of discovery may vary widely; that does not matter. The important thing is that the wood has depth and richness to reward a lifetime of quiet, perceptive searching.